MACHAUT

Oxford Studies of Composers

Roger Nichols: DEBUSSY
Denis Arnold: GIOVANNI GABRIELI
Ian Kemp: HINDEMITH
H. Wiley Hitchcock: IVES
Gilbert Reaney: MACHAUT
Denis Arnold: MARENZIO
Roger Nichols: MESSIAEN
Jerome Roche: PALESTRINA
Anthony Payne: SCHOENBERG
Norman Kay: SHOSTAKOVICH
Hugh Macdonald: SKRYABIN
Paul Doe: TALLIS
David Brown: WILBYE

Oxford Studies of Composers (9)

GUILLAUME DE MACHAUT

GILBERT REANEY

London

OXFORD UNIVERSITY PRESS

NEW YORK   MELBOURNE

Oxford University Press, Walton Street, Oxford OX2 6DP

OXFORD   LONDON   GLASGOW   NEW YORK
TORONTO   MELBOURNE   WELLINGTON   CAPE TOWN
IBADAN   NAIROBI   DAR ES SALAAM   LUSAKA
KUALA LUMPUR   SINGAPORE   JAKARTA   HONG KONG   TOKYO
DELHI   BOMBAY   CALCUTTA   MADRAS   KARACHI

ISBN 0 19 315218 5

© Oxford University Press 1971

First published 1971
Third impression 1978

Printed and bound in Great Britain at
The Camelot Press Ltd, Southampton

CONTENTS

Introduction   7

I   Machaut Musician-Poet   10

II   Machaut's Musical Style   18

III   The Lays and Virelais   30

IV   The Ballades and Rondeaux   39

V   The Motets   50

VI   The Mass and Hoquetus   60

Conclusion   69

Chronological Table   74

Bibliography   75

INTRODUCTION

The life of Guillaume de Machaut (*c.* 1300–77) spans the greater part of the fourteenth century, and in particular covers the Ars Nova period in its classic phase. Thanks to the researches of Armand Machabey,[1] his biography is now fairly well known. Machaut entered the service of John of Luxembourg, king of Bohemia, about 1323, and followed the king in his many campaigns throughout Europe. He was the king's secretary, a post which must have left him little time for composing, as he traversed Poland, Silesia, Lithuania, Bohemia and Italy between 1327 and 1330. During the next five years, however, he began to acquire the canonries which helped him to gain his independence. He was a canon of Reims, where he eventually settled in the 1340s, and also of St. Quentin, whose patron saint he honoured in the motet *Martyrum gemma latria–Diligenter inquiramus–A Christo honoratus* (19). Following John of Luxembourg's death at Crecy in 1346, Machaut was successively in the service of John's daughter Bonne (wife of the future King John II of France), King Charles the Bad of Navarre, Charles of Normandy (King of France from 1364) and Pierre I de Lusignan, King of Cyprus. Wealthy dukes like John of Berry and Amédée of Savoy also patronized him. These noble art-lovers particularly enjoyed hearing the long allegorical poems called *Dits* on dark winter evenings. Machaut himself wrote two of them for Charles of Navarre[2] and at least one for John of Berry[2] and Pierre de Lusignan[3] respectively.

[1] *Guillaume de Machault 130?–1377* I, p. 13.

[2] *Le Jugement du Roi de Navarre* and *Le Confort d'Ami* for Charles, and *La Fonteinne amoureuse* for John, all published in E. Hoepffner, *Oeuvres de Guillaume de Machaut* I, p. 137; III, p. 1, 143.

[3] *Le Prise d'Alexandrie*, ed. L. de Mas Latrie (Paris, 1876).

The last years of his life must have been occupied with putting the finishing touches to his complete works, which have been preserved in more or less complete state in six large manuscripts provided with musical notation.

Biographically much information can be derived from the *Voir Dit*, which Machabey dates between 1361 and 1365.[4] This so-called true story of the ageing poet's love for a nineteen-year-old girl, Péronne d'Armentières, has an air of authenticity, and in any case sheds much light on the composer's ideas and methods of composition.[5] Were polyphonic compositions written at one fell swoop? Not always, apparently, since Machaut mentions a Rondeau whose Cantus had been written some time before the Tenor and Contratenor.[6] Did he use well-known refrains as a basis for new compositions? It would seem so, since the Ballade *Nès que on porroit* (33) is based on its refrain *Le grand desir que j'ay de vous veoir*, as Péronne had requested.[7] Much more obscure is Machaut's early education. Possibly he grew up at Reims, where the name Wuillaume Machaux crops up in 1310,[8] though clearly this was an older man, perhaps Guillaume's father. Moreover, Machaut's earliest datable motet, *Bone pastor Guillerme—Bone pastor qui pastores* (18), was written for the election of Guillaume of Trie as archbishop of Reims in 1324. However, the musical technique is mature and the motet is placed toward the end of the motet fascicle in the complete manuscripts.

Medieval techniques, of course, tend to be considered the province of the specialist, which is why a separate chapter is devoted to Machaut's musical style in this volume. Even the hocket, that forerunner of syncopation whereby a rest on the

---

[4] *Guillaume de Machault* I, p. 56ff, and II, p. 173. The poem was published by P. Paris (Paris, 1875).

[5] The sections dealing with music are quoted by F. Ludwig, *Guillaume de Machaut, Musikalische Werke* II, p. 54ff.

[6] ibid., 56 (*Voir Dit*, letter 31, p. 242).

[7] ibid., 54 (*Voir Dit*, letter 6, p. 56).

[8] Machabey, *Guillaume de Machault* I, p. 18, and II, p. 171.

main beat creates the effect of syncopation on the offbeat, is foreign to more recent music. The numbers in parentheses following work titles refer to the numbers of compositions in the Schrade edition of Machaut's works. However, the Ludwig edition may sometimes be more useful for study purposes, where it indicates more exactly the rhythmic organization of a composition. The musical examples in the present volume may well vary from both these editions, if this seems necessary. The bibliography is selective but, hopefully, useful. The plainsong cited can be found in the *Liber Usualis*.

A guide to the chronology of the composition of Machaut's music is given by the principal manuscripts, which apparently followed the order the composer himself wanted.[9] Stylistic considerations and other factors, such as occurrence in the *Voir Dit*, are further aids in this complex study. The table given at the end is based on my own studies, as well as the invaluable work of Dr. Ursula Günther. Footnotes are only given where necessary, since the bibliography covers some of the references.

[9] See the rubric to the index of the ms Paris, Bibl. Nat. franc. 1584: *Vesci l'ordenance que G. de Machau met qu'il ait en son livre.*

I

MACHAUT MUSICIAN-POET

It is only recently that fourteenth-century poetry has been taken at its face value and therefore gained more appreciation. Previously it was often condemned as full of clichés and rhyme-play and lacking in depth.[1] Certainly it is true that the lyric poems were purely for the entertainment of the nobility, and the subject-matter therefore tended to be concerned with various aspects of love,[2] just as in popular songs today. Both music and poetry, which were not inevitably linked—Machaut himself wrote many lyric poems without music—were, to be sure, on a higher level aesthetically than the present-day popular song, but the need to entertain probably kept lyric song relatively superficial in content. The refinement lay metrically, in the form and versification and musically in rhythm and harmony. Melody, incidentally, was an aspect of harmony for the medieval composer, for consonance could involve the successive combination of intervals just as well as the simultaneous sounding of different notes.

Since pure instrumental music has not been preserved from the Middle Ages, with the exception of a few instrumental dances, medieval music is inextricably linked with a text, which means a poetic text, unless the words are taken from the traditional plainsong. Therefore, although it is quite possible

---

[1] See, for example, N. Wilkins, *One Hundred Ballades, Rondeaux and Virelais from the late Middle Ages* (Cambridge, 1969), p. vii; also J. Bédier and P. Hazard, *Littérature française* I, Paris 1948, p. 114f.

[2] See Reaney, 'Guillaume de Machaut: Lyric Poet', *Music and Letters* xxxix (1958), p. 40; also N. Wilkins, *One Hundred Ballades* . . ., p. 5.

for the music to be performed without the words, for example on instruments, the form of the music ultimately stems from the form of the poem being set. This is perhaps not quite so much the case with the motet, which depends on a Tenor borrowed from a plainsong melisma and set out in rigidly organized rhythmic patterns and phrases. Only the upper parts usually have poetic texts, and these are less regular than the song forms.

Particularly important for the latter is the long narrative poem called the *Remède de Fortune*, usually dated before 1349.[3] It is a rambling love story, in which the poet manages to give examples of the principal types of lyric song he composed (Lay, Ballade, Rondeau and Virelai, but also the less common Chanson Royal and Complainte).[4] The Lay in the story was his undoing, since he had written it in praise of his lady, and she somehow came across the manuscript. Not knowing whose it was, she asked him to read it, but when she enquired who was the author, he could not answer and fled. This resulted in the Complainte, in which he cursed the cruelty of Fortune, together with the personification of Love, the source of his miseries. Another personification, as usual a woman of great beauty, appears and counters all the poet's arguments. This is Hope, and she ends the first part of her speech with the Chanson Royal. Shortly afterwards she sings the so-called Baladelle. In both pieces she praises Love, and the poet is cheered, so much so that he himself composes the Ballade with music and a poem of thanks called a *prière*, this time without notation. He goes back to find the beloved dancing, and, like the others, sings a song to accompany the dancing, a Virelai. Having con-

---

[3] Günther, *Der musikalische Stilwandel . . .*, p. 18; idem, *Acta Musicologica* xxxv (1963), p. 100. The *Remède* is published by E. Hoepffner, *Oeuvres de Guillaume de Machaut* II, p. 1.

[4] All published in the principal editions of Ludwig, *Guillaume de Machaut, Musikalische Werke*, I, p. 93, and Schrade, *Polyphonic Music of the Fourteenth Century* II, p. 102, 106, 107; III, p. 138, 140, 166, 192; also as an appendix to the Hoepffner volume in a transcription by Ludwig.

fessed to the lady that he wrote the Lay, she agrees to accept him as her *ami*. Then follows a graphic description of a day in the life of a big château, at the end of which the poet is dismissed in a friendly fashion and exchanges rings with his lady. His joy inspires him to compose a Rondeau, which he sings as he departs. It is not surprising that this is the last of the songs, for he receives no encouragement on his next visit. The lady is cool to him, but explains it away as necessary when slanderers are about. The poem ends with further praise of Love.

The seven lyric works interpolated in the *Remède de Fortune* are not included in the complete collections of Machaut's poems. Thus, they were doubtless composed specially for the *Remède*, and indeed Machaut himself calls the Chanson Royal a *chant nouvel* and says that the Baladelle is *de chant et de dittié nouvelle*.[5] Only in the case of the Virelai does he say nothing about the time of composition. It would seem that Machaut wanted to give a conspectus of the musico-poetic forms of his time, for two of them he never set again, namely the Complainte and the Chanson Royal, though the final Ballade *Ma douce dame* in the main collection is in the Complainte form rather than the standard Ballade form.

The Lay is in the usual twelve-stanza form of the fourteenth century.[6] Each of these stanzas is divided into two equal parts, and often four, each of which is sung to the same music. The final stanza is the same as the first, musically and in poetic form, but the inner stanzas can be extremely varied. Like the Virelai, the Lay often uses short lines and variety of line-length, not to mention frequently repeated rhymes, and all of this is closely followed by the more or less note-against-note musical setting. Here, for example, is stanza 10, with the verse-scheme $a_4a_4a_4a_4a_8b_6$ (Ex. 1).

Lays are unusual in having eleven different stanzas of music,

<hr>

[5] Ludwig I, p. 97f (*Remède*, lines 1984 and 2852).
[6] See chapter III, p. 30.

but the other forms use the same music for each stanza. The Complainte is almost excessive in this respect, for it has thirty-six strophes, all repeating the same music.[7] The stanza form is $a_8a_8a_8b_4$, $a_8a_8a_8b_4$, $b_8b_8b_8a_4$, $b_8b_8b_8a_4$. Musically, however, the work is fairly syllabic and similar to the Lay in its use of a straightforward $\frac{3}{4}$ time.

A close relation of the Ballade, the Chanson Royal still harks back to the thirteenth century *chansons*.[8] It has an *envoi*, i.e. three concluding lines which are sung to the last three musical phrases and correspond to the last three lines of each stanza. These were also composed for Ballades, but they do not appear in Machaut's settings. Similarly, the lack of a refrain is another archaic feature, as well as the use of lines varying in length from five to ten syllables. Otherwise, there are five stanzas instead of the Ballade's usual three. In the music, too, there are archaic features, traces of the old rhythmic modes, for instance (the third: ♩ ♪ ♩, the fourth: ♪ ♪ ♩. etc.).

[7] Complete poem in E. Hoepffner. *Oeuvres . . . de Machaut* II, p. 33.

[8] Cf. the chansons of Adam de la Hale (new edition by N. Wilkins, *The Lyric Works of Adam de la Hale* (Tübingen, 1967), p. 3).

The importance of the two Ballades, the Rondeau and the Virelai is shown by the fact that these are preserved in many more manuscripts than the other song-forms, as well as by the three- and four-part writing for the Ballade and Rondeau. Machaut exemplifies the two principal musical variants of the Ballade in the *Remède*. The first, called a Baladelle, has first and second time bars at the end of both sections of the composition, giving an overall AABB form, but this form is rarely used. The form of the poem is also divided into four parts, namely twelve lines divided into four three-line sections, with

the scheme $\underbrace{a_7 a_3 b_7}_{A} \underbrace{a_7 a_3 b_7}_{A} \underbrace{b_7 b_3 a_7}_{B} \underbrace{b_7 b_3 A_7}_{B}.$ Although the musical

setting involves Cantus, Tenor, Contratenor and textless Triplum, it is none too modern in style with its $\frac{9}{8}$ rhythm and harmonically dissonant fourth part (the Triplum). The more typical Ballade *Dame de qui toute ma joie vient* exemplifies the AAB form with three eight-line stanzas, each having the

scheme $\underbrace{a_{10} b_{10}}_{A} \underbrace{a_{10} b_{10}}_{A} \underbrace{c_7 c_{10} d_{10} D_{10}}_{B}.$ The modernity of this verse-

form is immediately obvious from its use of lines of identical length, except for the variant short line of seven syllables, which was standard in the eight-line stanza. Strangely enough, Machaut does not give an example of the equally popular seven-line stanza, though this is essentially the same as the eight-line strophe without the short line. The music of *Dame de qui* is just as modern as the stanza, for it is in $\frac{3}{4}$ time and has frequent syncopations. Moreover, the four-part harmony is rather more successful than in the Baladelle.

Like the Lay, the Virelai form tends to great variety of versification, but once again Machaut's *Remède* example is the form he most often uses, though musically it is monophonic. Another name for the Virelay was *chanson baladée*, and Machaut maintained that this was the proper name for it,[9] but this secondary designation was soon dropped in the course of the century. Like the Ballade, the Virelai at the time of Machaut consists of three stanzas, but whereas the Ballade stanza usually falls into the pattern AAB, that of the Virelai is ABBAA, because the Refrain appears at the beginning and end of each stanza. The similarity between the two forms becomes more apparent if the Virelai is divided up into Refrain-AA-B (to Refrain music)- Refrain. In the Ballade the refrain amounts to no more than a single line of text at the end of each strophe, so that it is incorporated in the B section. Machaut's

Virelai in the *Remède* has the stanza form $\underbrace{A_7A_7B_4B_7A_4A_7B_4}_{A}$ $\underbrace{b_7b_7a_4}_{B}\underbrace{b_7b_7a_4}_{B}\underbrace{a_7a_7b_4b_7a_4a_7b_4}_{A}$, etc.[10]

Finally, the Rondeau is in the eight-line form typical of the thirteenth and fourteenth century, though the use of lines equal in length and particularly the decasyllabic line so favoured by Machaut reveals its modernity. The repetitions of the music, and indeed of the refrain text, are one of the most obvious features of the Rondeau, which however gradually became more sophisticated. In the eight-line form only one line of text was sung to each complete section of the music, but soon, and to some extent already in the works of Machaut, the refrain, and consequently the remaining parts of the verse became textually longer. Thus, although the standard form is A B a A a b A B , with each line of text corresponding to each section of the music, we also find Machaut writing $\frac{\text{AB B ab AB ab b AB B}}{\text{A B A A A B A B}}$ in three Rondeaux.

The plot of the *Remède de Fortune* gives a good idea of the

[9] Ludwig I, p. 101 (*Remède*, lines 3447–50).
[10] Reaney, *Musica Disciplina* xiii (1959), p. 35.

type of subject-matter to be found in the lyric poems. The much later *Voir Dit* is an entirely different matter. The artificial story gives way to a personal narrative in which the poet mingles letters and songs with the narrative poetry. The use of songs in this work is quite different from the didactic plan of the *Remède*. Here the songs are part of the narrative or at least a commentary on the plot. Moreover, they exist independently of the *Voir Dit* in the complete collections of music to be found in the complete Machaut manuscripts. All are in the modern Ballade or Rondeau form, with the exception of the Lay. There are four Virelai poems,[11] but Machaut never set them to music.

While the *Voir Dit* is basically the story of how the poet came to know Péronne and fall in love with her, it is much more than that. Clearly the young girl's interest in the sixty-year-old poet was mainly his verse and music, but he seemed unable to realize this. He was dazzled by her, and even when he heard rumours of her fickleness, did not believe them. Finally she tired of him, and even then he seemed unable to read between the lines of her letters. It is clear that the true part of the story ends here, and, although Machaut concludes by saying that he and Péronne continued to live and love happily, we may be sure that in reality she never saw him again. This human side of the poem is extremely apparent in the interchange of letters between the two lovers, which also gives a unique insight into the nature of Machaut's methods of composition. He sends Péronne the Ballade *Nès que on porroit* (33), which he says is in the style of a German composition. He asks her to get to know it as it is, without adding or taking away anything, and also says that the piece is in very long measures, presumably referring to the $\frac{6}{8}$ rhythm. In a rare hint at instrumentation, he adds that, for anyone who can play the piece on the organ, bagpipes or other instruments, this is its very nature. Since Péronne keeps asking Guillaume to send

[11] See Chichmaref II, p. 610, 625, 626, 628; P. Paris, *Le Voir Dit*, p. 72, 39, 37, 38.

her his manuscripts, he says he would do this, but the book which contains his complete compositions is in more than twenty pieces, because he is having it notated, and in any case it is being written for one of his princely patrons. But when it is notated, he will bring or send it to her. Of the Rondeau *Dix et sept* (17), which is an anagram on Péronne's name, Guillaume says he will send the music as soon as he can, so that it is clear that music and text were not composed simultaneously. And in the case of the Ballade *Quant Theseus—Ne quier veoir* (34), he is quite explicit in modestly saying that the first text was written by Thomas Paien, to which he replied in the same metre and rhyme with *Ne quier veoir*. Once again Péronne has to wait for the music, but eventually he writes it in four parts, and undoubtedly it is one of his best works. There are eight pieces altogether with musical notation in the *Voir Dit*, but after *Quant Theseus—Ne quier veoir* Machaut only writes one further composition in the *Voir Dit*, namely the Ballade *Se pour ce muir* (36) in which he complains that his lady is betraying him. And shortly before, he writes that, because he is so melancholy, he will never more compose a Ballade, Rondeau, Virelai or Lay.[12]

[12] Ludwig II, p. 58 (*Voir Dit*, lines 7537–44).

MACHAUT'S MUSICAL STYLE

Even today an assessment of the style of any medieval music is by no means easy, but serious studies and fairly frequent performance have at least made the task more approachable. The very thought of fourteenth-century French music conjures up such works of Machaut as the Mass, the Virelai *Douce dame jolie* (4) and the Ballade *Je puis trop bien* (28). And yet these works are all rather different from each other, in spite of the appearance of some typical Machaut motifs in all of them. It would seem that difference of purpose and difference of form resulted in specific styles. With the exception of the Mass and the Hoquetus *David*, and possibly the six Latin motets, Machaut's music was secular. The French motets were based on Latin tenors for the most part, and in some cases could conceivably have been used in connection with the worship of the Virgin Mary, but essentially the texts of the upper voices are love-songs.

As might be expected, the works in more than one part tend to be in a different style from the monodies, but this is not always the case. For instance, the one unaccompanied Ballade by Machaut, *Dame, se vous m'estes lonteinne* (37), has the typical $\frac{6}{8}$ rhythm and the many auxiliary notes typical of so many of the Ballades and Rondeaux. But in general the solos are much more syllabic than the polyphonic songs. The Lays and Virelais are in this category, and of course both forms date back to the thirteenth century.[1] Pieces in duple time and pro-

[1] See Maillard; and F. Gennrich, *Rondeaux, Virelais und Balladen*, 2 vols., (Dresden 1921–7).

lation, i.e. $\frac{2}{4}$ or $\frac{4}{4}$, naturally sound more modern than those in the triplets of $\frac{6}{8}$ and $\frac{9}{8}$ because, triple time predominated in the thirteenth century; but also there is a folk-like flavour in them untypical of Machaut and the fourteenth century. This is particularly true of works without much ornamentation, like *Douce dame jolie* (4) and *Quant je sui mis au retour* (13) (Ex. 2).

Ex. 2

Quant je   sui mis   au   re – tour   de ve – oir   ma da – me

These are both Virelais, but, although common time is less frequent in the Lays, they too have their folk-like passages. The main difference between the two forms is in fact poetic rather than musical, apart from the fact that the Lay has greater scope for variety and expansion.

Contrasting sharply with the syllabic style is a melismatic type of writing which predominates in most of Machaut's polyphonic works. This is partly the result of spreading out many notes over relatively short texts, a feature almost bound to occur in the Rondeaux, where only two lines of text take up the entire composition. The other lines simply repeat the first or second phrase of the music. A style which falls in between the two principal ones is a syllabic texture with short melismas, such as occurs in the Lay *Par trois raisons* (5) (Ex. 3).

Ex. 3

Par   trois rai – sons me   vueil def – –   ten – dre
de   m'a – mour, qui ja –   –   mais n'iert   men – dre,

Although these ornamental motifs may seem to be introduced in a rather artificial fashion, they nevertheless form an extremely effective means of textural organization. The melismatic style may seem arbitrary and far removed from our own methods of musical construction, but a closer examination reveals that, in spite of the asymmetrical rhythms, a very rational arrangement of constantly varied motifs underlies the melody as a whole. The frequent use of syncopation, rests and relatively lengthy phrases is a little disconcerting, after more recent music, but a realization of the craftsmanship of the composer is likely to produce admiration for this lost art. In the polyphonic Ballades and Rondeaux, and even the simpler Virelais, it is usually the Cantus part which is the most developed, as one might expect, rather than the accompanying textless voices. Here for instance is the eight-bar melisma concluding Machaut's motet-like Ballade *Quant Theseus—Ne quier veoir* (34) in the second Cantus part (Ex. 4).

Ex. 4

In two-part songs the accompaniment is a Tenor moving generally an octave or a fifth below the Cantus, while in three-part works a further part moving in the Tenor range and called Contratenor is added. Occasionally this may be replaced by a Triplum, also textless and moving in the Cantus range or higher. Four-part works have both Contratenor and Triplum, but in some cases the basic texture is three-part with either Contratenor or Triplum and not both, as in the Ballade *De Fortune* (23). *Quant Theseus—Ne quier veoir* is an exceptional case, for the textless Triplum is replaced by a second Cantus part.

Machaut's polyphonic songs are the earliest solo songs extant with written-out accompaniments, though we may assume that Troubadour and Trouvère songs had improvised instrumental accompaniments, and two-part thirteenth-century motets with Tenors consisting of measured plainsong melismas set to French upper parts may have had a similar function.[2] The accompanying parts sometimes take part in the motivic interplay, but the Tenors are usually simpler than the vocal part. The Contratenor may be closely linked rhythmically with the Tenor, but some of the most interesting Contratenor parts are very lively—full of leaps and syncopations and repeated notes suggestive of improvisation. A good example is the Contratenor of the Ballade *De Fortune*, which is particularly animated in the version found in the codex written for the Duke of Berry[3] (Ex. 5.)

Ex. 5

Both Lays and Virelais, though mainly monodic, may be polyphonic, but the Lays have no textless parts. Two of them are canonic, one throughout and one in alternate verses, the other verse being monodic. The other two are notated as monodies, but combine in the one case each half stanza in two-part harmony, and in the other every three stanzas in three-part harmony. *Pour ce que plus proprement* is remarkable for its perfect note-against-note writing[4] (Ex. 6). With one exception, the polyphonic Virelais are two-part works with a

Ex. 6

[2] Reaney, 'The Middle Ages', *A History of Song*, ed. D. Stevens (London, 1960), p. 42; idem, 'The Performance of Medieval Music', *Aspects of Medieval and Renaissance Music* (New York, 1966), p. 715.

[3] Paris, Bibl. Nat., franç. 9221, f.151.

[4] Transcription by Hoppin, *Musica Disciplina* xii (1958), p. 96.

simple textless Tenor. *Très bonne et belle, mi oueil* (23) also has a textless Contratenor, which is in much the same rhythmic style as the Tenor.

The other principal type of polyphonic composition cultivated by Machaut is the motet. It appears to be less at the centre of his production than the polyphonic songs, but we may assume that he wrote many of the French motets in a first flush of success as an Ars Nova composer, then making the transition from the motet to the accompanied solo song. Certainly many of the motets have a style reminiscent of the latest motets in the *Roman de Fauvel*, which was completed by 1316. If we compare the opening of *Aman novi probatur—Heu, Fortuna subdola—Heu me, tristis*[5] from the Fauvel manuscript with Machaut's *De Bon Espoir—Puis que la douce—Speravi* (4), it is clear that the rhythms and even the melodic line of the upper parts are much the same in both works. One reason for this was that the early Ars Nova motet tended to stick to a restricted number of motifs, rhythmic or melodic as well, in a trochaic subdivision of $\frac{6}{8}$ time. The fourteenth-century motet is often said to be a conservative work, even though it introduced the concept of isorhythm or at least developed it dramatically. It was conservative in that it continued a thirteenth-century form, and stuck to trochaic rhythms. Three of Machaut's motets (11, 16, 20) are even more conservative in abandoning isorhythm and employing a secular song as the Tenor, though they do make some use of iambic rhythms.

Isorhythm is in reality just one of the many means of formal organization used in medieval musical composition. It is a modern term coined to express the technique whereby motets and sometimes other forms employed lengthy passages of music identical with each other in rhythm if not in pitch. The medieval term *color* covered this meaning as well as others, since it referred to any kind of pattern.[6] However,

[5] Schrade, I, p. 48.   [6] Reaney, 'Color', *MGG* ii, col. 1574.

modern writers seem to have been particularly attracted by the terms *color* and *talea* used by Johannes de Muris in the mid-1320s and particularly suited to the type of motet which has melodic and rhythmic repetitions which do not coincide. For instance, Machaut's *Fons totius—O livoris* (9)[7] has a Tenor whose rhythmic pattern is repeated three times to every two statements of the melody. Actually the situation is slightly complicated by the fact that the first note of the melody does not enter on the first beat of the isorhythmic period, and this causes a corresponding overlap into the first measure of the second *color*, and all succeeding odd *colores*. Machaut's artistry is revealed by the fact that the even *colores* do begin on the first beat of a *modus* group, and the overlap enables the Tenor melody to be used to the very final chord. Here are the first three *taleae* of the Tenor. The double bars indicate the end of each *talea* and the asterisk the beginning of each *color* (Ex. 7).

Ex. 7

Isorhythm was mainly used in the slow-moving Tenors, and in four-part works in the Contratenors, of Machaut's motets, but it also affected the upper parts to some degree, mainly in rhythmically interesting passages. The use of rests, hocket and occasionally syncopation seemed to demand isorhythm.[8] The opening four measures of each *talea* of the Triplum and Motetus parts of *Fons totius—O livoris* are isorhythmic, though as usual the first *talea* is a little different from the others.

The use of *modus* groups in the motet is one of the conservative features it retained from the thirteenth century. Already around the year 1300 the introduction of many shorter

[7] See Eggebrecht. [8] Günther, *Musica Disciplina* xii (1958), 31.

notes into the upper parts of motets helped to make the Tenors longer. *Modus* was the relation of long to breve, and in the Notre Dame school of *c.* 1200 these two notes represented the equivalent of quite rapidly moving crotchets and quavers in $\frac{3}{8}$ or $\frac{6}{8}$ time. But in 1300, although the terminology was the same, it was the breve and semibreve that moved at the speed of the long and breve of 1200. By the second decade of the fourteenth century it had become necessary to clarify the relationships between increasingly shorter note-values and the older, longer note-values. Thus, Philippe de Vitry and Johannes de Muris distinguished *modus* from *tempus*, the relation between breve and semibreve, and *tempus* from *prolatio*, the relation between semibreve and minim.[9] These different levels of measurement, which seem rather unnecessary, nowadays all fall under the heading of time. In the isorhythmic motet, however, the different degrees of mensuration found simultaneous practical fulfilment, with mode predominating in the lower parts and time and prolation in the upper ones.[10] And yet this new form had much in common with the Notre Dame organa in three and four parts: the long notes in the Tenor, the trochaic rhythms of the upper parts, and the heightening of tension by the speeding up of the Tenor towards the end.

Another big innovation heralded by Philippe de Vitry and Johannes de Muris was the equivalence of duple and triple rhythms in all combinations. In the thirteenth century, duple rhythm had been considered as lacking the perfection of triple and was called imperfect, but with the advent of the Ars

[9] Ph. de Vitry, 'Ars perfecta' in C. E. H. de Coussemaker, *Scriptorum de musica medii aevi nova series* III (Paris, 1869), p. 29; Joh. de Muris, 'Libellus cantus mensurabilis', ibid., p. 47.

[10] A further degree of length is also found in the isorhythmic motet at times, namely the all-encompassing *maximodus*, in which the already lengthy *modus* measures may occupy half or a third of a *maximodus* measure. Thus, if time and prolation are respectively duple and triple ($\frac{6}{8}$), and *modus* is duple (making $\frac{12}{8}$ altogether), triple *maximodus* would give an overriding measure of three $\frac{12}{8}$ *modus* bars.

24

Nova, *c.* 1320, this stigma was removed[11]—even though the conservative theorist Jacobus of Liège rails at the use of imperfections by the moderns in his *Speculum musicae*[12] written *c.* 1325. Even so, such combinations as duple time and duple prolation ($\frac{2}{4}$ or $\frac{4}{4}$) were less frequent than duple time and triple prolation ($\frac{6}{8}$) or triple time and duple prolation ($\frac{3}{4}$) in the fourteenth century.

Guillaume de Machaut is often considered to be the first composer of a complete polyphonic Mass, with the possible exception of the contemporary Tournai Mass,[13] and certainly previous compositions were usually restricted to individual movements, such as the two-part Kyries in the eleventh-century Winchester Troper.[14] But this is probably to over-estimate the importance of the Mass Ordinary in the Middle Ages. It was unnecessary to link together movements which were liturgically separated, such as Gloria, Credo and Sanctus. Only with the fourteenth century was there a systematic attempt, even in plainsong settings, to link the fixed texts of the Mass Ordinary together. Polyphony in any case was not re-quired except on special occasions, as in votive masses, and it seems clear that Machaut's Mass was a Lady Mass, for it is called *la messe de nostre dame* in the manuscript New York, Wildenstein Collection, f. 283v. That the Mass Ordinary was a relative newcomer to the polyphonic scene is shown by the variety of forms it borrows in the fourteenth century, without having any specific form of its own. Machaut uses isorhythmic motet form in the Kyrie, Sanctus, Agnus and Ite, while the Gloria and Credo, with their much longer texts, have an elaborated note-against-note style. He also uses duple prola-tion throughout, which gives the work a modern touch, also

---

[11] See note 9.

[12] Coussemaker, *Scriptorum* . . . II, p. 427f.

[13] Modern editions by Ch. van den Borren, *Missa Tornacensis* (Haarlem, 1957); Schrade I, p. 110.

[14] Cambridge, Corpus Christi College, ms 473.

evident perhaps in the four-part writing. For an example of the rather strange harmonies see Ex. 8.

Ex. 8

The Hoquetus *David* stands apart from the rest of Machaut's production, though its Tenor is isorhythmic and hocket is not infrequent in motets as well. This work is the last in a line of thirteenth-century compositions whose two upper parts were textless and which exploited the possibilities of hocket technique. The *modus* notation and $\frac{9}{8}$ rhythm give an archaic quality to the work which is heightened by the frequent parallel fifths. The complexity of the piece becomes clear when one realizes that both upper voices take part in the hocketing, and the Tenor as well in the first part of the composition.

The tonal system of medieval music[15] is still something of a mystery, partly because the theorists of the time never talk about this aspect of part-music, or even monodic secular music. Tonality, or modality, was clearly based on the church modes employed in plainsong, basically a series of octaves, the Dorian extending from D, the Phrygian from E, the Lydian from F, and the Mixolydian from G, together with the so-called plagal modes a fourth lower. The latter were related to

[15] See Reaney, 'Modes in the Fourteenth Century, in particular in the Music of Guillaume de Machaut', *Organicae voces* (*Festschrift Joseph Smits van Waesberghe*) (Amsterdam, 1963), p. 137.

the former, the so-called authentic modes, by having the same final note or tonic, but consisted of a lower fourth and upper fifth instead of a lower fifth and upper fourth. Thus, the Hypodorian stretched an octave from A and ended on D, and the other plagals followed the same plan. This was not the whole story, however, for it is only necessary to look at the music of Machaut to realize that many pieces end on C, and, apart from a few apparently out-of-place accidentals, give the impression of being in C major. The Ballade *Nes que on porroit* (33) and the Rondeau *Rose liz* (10), are good examples, for they both begin and end on a chord of C. Even in these passages, however, there are what today would be considered touches of the minor mode in the introduction of B flat in descending passages. It is evident that such 'secular' modes did not fit comfortably into the framework of ecclesiastical music, and even in the early sixteenth century, theorists like Pietro Aron were still trying to fit them into the pattern of the transposed Mixolydian.

Polyphonic music made new demands on the modal system. The necessity of having single parts at different levels was the reason why fifteenth-century theorists like Tinctoris[16] considered that each voice should be considered separately as to its mode, though the basic voice, if the mode of the entire piece was to be assessed, was the Tenor. The complication is that the basic harmonic interval in part-music is the fifth, which has to be perfect, and in certain positions cannot be so without the addition of accidentals, e.g. between the notes B and F. An easy way of seeing that this diminished fifth was always perfect was to have a flat in the clef of the Tenor in two-part writing, often in the Contratenor as well in three or four parts. This was Machaut's usual method, which to some extent accounts for the so-called partial signatures, in which certain parts, usually the lower ones, had flat signatures, while the

[16] Coussemaker, *Scriptorum* . . . IV, 1876, p. 29.

other voices had less or none.[17] Also involved, however, was the concept of transposition, well-known previously in plainsong. Thus, the Dorian mode could be transposed to G or C by one or two flats in the Tenor clef. This was the medieval minor, while the unecclesiastical major on C could be transposed to F and B flat.

An element of mystery also surrounds the harmony of late medieval music. Just as medieval theorists do not bother to discuss modality in polyphonic music, neither do they consider it necessary to talk about florid counterpoint. Yet it is clear that most of Machaut's music is florid to a degree. The theorists of course tend to be discussing elementary theory. They list the basic intervals and tell us what progressions can be made in two-part writing. There are three degrees of consonance at this time: perfect consonance, imperfect consonance, and true dissonance. Generally speaking, these involve (a) the octave, unison, and fifth, (b) the third and sixth, and (c) the second, fourth, and seventh. As principal harmonies, the third and sixth seem to have almost acquired the rights of the perfect consonances, but still gravitate to and from the perfect intervals. Dissonances are used mostly in passing, but in florid counterpoint such as Machaut's, as compared with note-against-note movement, the dissonance technique is extremely complex and developed. In part this was caused by the use of the conventional motifs mentioned earlier (see p. 19) but also by syncopation, particularly in duple rhythms. The addition of a third or fourth voice complicated the issue considerably, as can be seen from the opening of Machaut's Rondeau *Tant doucement* (9) (Ex. 9). Even without the Contratenor or Triplum, seconds, fourths, and sevenths are created by the syncopated vocal part. The Contratenor too is

---

[17] See R. H. Hoppin, 'Partial Signatures and Musica Ficta in Some Early 15th-Century Sources', *Journal of the American Musicological Society* vi (1953), p. 197; E. E. Lowinsky, 'The Functions of Conflicting Signatures in Early Polyphonic Music', *Musical Quarterly* xxxi (1945), p. 227.

Ex. 9

very syncopated, and even though the Triplum is carefully harmonized with the Contratenor when the latter is beneath the Tenor, the total result is harmonies like the seventh DFAC and more complex formations involving parallel sevenths or ninths. In particular, the simultaneous performance of different kinds of conventional motif, e.g. an escape-note motif plus regular passing notes, tends to produce dissonance.

III

THE LAYS AND VIRELAIS

It comes as rather a surprise to find that Machaut wrote no less than nineteen Lays, in spite of the model Lay in the *Remède de Fortune*, since other monophonic forms like the Complainte and the Chanson Royal were apparently less interesting to him. Admittedly Machaut did introduce polyphony into four Lays, but the form is nevertheless first and foremost that of a one-line melody. If the *Roman de Fauvel* influenced Machaut's motets, it may have influenced his Lays too, since the source contains four splendid works in this form.[1] Two of them already have the regular twelve-stanza form of Machaut's Lays, instead of the irregular shape of earlier Lays. The rhythmic scheme harks back to the six rhythmic modes, as one might expect, but Machaut is much more advanced. He sometimes introduces such modernities as duple time and prolation, but this is evidently a late feature occurring primarily in the *Lay de la rose* (15) and the Lay *En demantant et lamentant* (18). The earlier Lays, however, are often written in the older notation consisting primarily of longs and breves, like the Fauvel Lays. Machaut's last Lay is an interesting case, for the opening stanza (transposed a fourth down to end the piece) is in the third rhythmic mode. It may be a borrowed melody, but at all events it contrasts strikingly with the more modern duple rhythms employed in much of the remainder of the piece. More recently Thomas Walker and Margaret Hasselman[2]

[1] See Reaney, *Proceedings of the Royal Musical Association* lxxxii, p. 21; also Maillard, p. 320.
[2] *Musica Disciplina* xxiv, p. 7.

discovered that the work was polyphonic, and that the first three stanzas, as well as succeeding groups of three strophes, combined in three-part harmony (Ex. 10).

Ex. 10

Even Machaut does not always have twelve stanzas of text. The second of his Lays, *J'aim la flour*, has only seven while the first Lay, *Loyauté que point ne delay*, although it has twelve strophes, has the same melody throughout, conflicting with the Lay principle of continual musical change. This variety, which incidentally makes for unusually long compositions, is what gives the Lay its great musical interest. It alone of the secular song forms is through-composed, with the exception of the repeat of the first stanza at the end, and even this is often transposed up or down a fourth or fifth. The other name for the Lay was the Descort, and any element of variety was considered a dis-cordant feature, i.e. discordant in the sense that it helped to produce the change desired in this form. Variety of poetic form and versification is evident in the constantly changing line-lengths and rhymes. A particularly striking case is the third Machaut Lay, *Pour ce qu'on puist mieus retraire*, which has lines of two to eight syllables, but only in one stanza the decasyllabic line typical of the fourteenth-century Ballade and Rondeau. As in most of the Lays, the length of the individual lines dictates the length of the melodic phrase. Here, in addition, however, the rhythmic identity between the lines of individual stanzas is often complete. This applies entirely to stanzas 3, 8, 10, and 11, and partially to stanzas 5, 6, and 9. In spite of the prevailing division of stanzas into two or four parts, stanzas 5 and 6 have a further formal procedure of interest which may be called ternary, i.e. the first phrase or the first two phrases are repeated at the end of the stanza.

In some Lays the twelve stanzas are clearly divided up into a symmetrical pattern. Perhaps the most obvious case is the canonic twelfth Lay, *S'onques douleureusement*, which is made up of three groups of four stanzas. The outer two groups are in $\frac{6}{8}$, the inner one in $\frac{3}{4}$, all of them apparently regulated by imperfect *modus*. Another obvious case is Lay 18, *En demantant et lamentant*, with its four groups of three stanzas, each group combining in three-part harmony. Even the use of polyphony involves an element of variety, for the first canonic Lay, *Je ne cesse de prier* (11), is monophonic in the odd stanzas and in three-part canon at the unison in the even stanzas, while *S'onques douleureusement* is canonic throughout, again at the unison and in three parts. Similarly, Lay 17, *Pour ce que plus proprement*,[3] contrasts with the three-part harmony of *En demantant* by its two-part note-against-note counterpoint, which Richard Hoppin discovered by placing the second half of each stanza underneath the first half. Both canonic Lays, however, are united by the subtle use of hocket, which is especially emphasized in the isorhythmic stanza 10 of Lay 12. The triple time syncopation is a novelty in Machaut which heralds the complexities of the late fourteenth century (Ex. 11).

The more typical monophonic Lay tends to move in $\frac{6}{4}$ or $\frac{6}{8}$ throughout, stressing the use of internal rhyme or short lines which combine as one longer line. Musically the internal rhyme is indicated by sequence, usually rhythmic but also melodic. A

[3] Transcription in *Musica Disciplina* xii, p. 96.

Ex. 11

good example is stanza 10 of Lay 7, *Amis, t'amour me contreint*, which moves isorhythmically and can be considered as an instance of the old sixth rhythmic mode (Ex. 12). In Lay 6,

Ex. 12

Amours doucement me tente, there is more variation of time and prolation between stanzas. Stanzas 1, 2, 4, and of course 12 are in $\frac{3}{4}$, stanzas 3, 9, 10, and 11 in $\frac{2}{4}$, and stanzas 5, 6, 7, and 8 in $\frac{6}{8}$. Once again, therefore, there is a strong tendency toward a triple division of the entire work into three groups of four stanzas, though this is offset by having a $\frac{2}{4}$ stanza among the $\frac{3}{4}$ group and the final $\frac{3}{4}$ stanza following the $\frac{2}{4}$ group.

The tonality of the Lays[4] is particularly interesting because

[4] See Reaney, *Proceedings of the Royal Musical Association* lxxxii, p. 29.

of the length of this type of composition. Ballades, Rondeaux and Virelais can be divided into two principal sections, but the Lay falls into at least twelve. This means that, although some Lays move within the same tonal area throughout, others modulate. For example, the Lay *Nuls ne doit avoir merveille* (4) moves from F with a B flat in the clef up to C, then repeating the process. In stanza 10 most of the movement is around the G a fifth higher, involving a B flat as the highest note. Stanza 11 has the same compass, but with the final on C; the piece ends with the musical repeat of stanza 1 a fifth higher than at the beginning, hence on C again. The suspicion that more than one singer may be involved in the performance of a single Lay is strengthened by the discovery that one clef is used for the first half of a Lay and a different one for the second half, in this case a Tenor followed by an Alto clef. In such an event, the transposition of the first stanza at the end of the piece has real justification. Although it is generally assumed that absolute pitch did not exist in the Middle Ages, the greater use of instruments in the fourteenth century and the increased use of accidentals may have paved the way for more fixed pitch levels.

The conservative nature of the Lays is indicated by the separation of each line of text from the next by a rest in most cases. However, especially in later works, short text lines are often joined to form one continuous phrase, as in the eighth stanza of Lay 8, where two three-syllable lines form one six-syllable line (Ex. 13). Lay 15, a later piece in duple rhythms,

Ex. 13

extends this process a little further. For instance, two eight-syllable lines form a single musical phrase in stanza 7, while a decasyllable is joined to a four-syllable line in stanza 9. The

Virelais, however, show these joins from the outset, even though they appear in many cases to be simple monophonic pieces. Only eight out of thirty-three Virelais are polyphonic, and all but one of these have no more than a simple Tenor in addition to the Cantus part. The one exception has a Contratenor as well. Both Lays and Virelais have short lines and varied line-lengths in the poetry, while the musical setting has predominantly one note per syllable. In his earliest Virelais, Machaut had relatively short stanzas of 10 or 12 lines (excluding the repeat of the refrain), but later expanded the strophes to as many as 21 or 22 lines of text.[5] As in the Lays, melismatic ornamentation tends to occur at cadential points, but is also found elsewhere. In Virelai 4, *Douce dame jolie*, a work in duple time and prolation, the ornamentation is restricted entirely to the cadence, usually in the form of the basic syncopated motif ♪ ♩ ♪. With triple prolation, especially in iambic settings reminiscent of the second rhythmic mode, the long note is often divided into two short ones. An example is the opening of Virelai 2, which also lengthens its first two syllables into dotted crotchets (originally semibreves) (Ex. 14).

Ex. 14

The importance of the use of first and second time bars (*ouvert* and *clos* in medieval terms) at the end of the two principal sections of the Virelai was first noticed by Ursula Günther.[6]

[5] Reaney, *Musica Disciplina* xiii, p. 35.

[6] *Der musikalische Stilwandel* . . ., p. 56; *Acta Musicologica* xxxv (1963), p. 110. The German words Stollen and Abgesang are often used for sections bb and a of the Virelai scheme AbbaA, where A is the Refrain.

Machaut, as might be expected, makes use of all possible combinations, but it is clear that the earlier idea was to have first and second time bars for the refrain section principally, and sometimes for the Stollen section as well. Later, this plan changed, and the polyphonic Virelais in particular tend to have a through-composed refrain with first and second time bars for the Stollen only. Another possibility, the complete elimination of first and second time bars, was less popular, but occurs in as late a work as the polyphonic Virelai *En mon cuer a un descort* (24).

In works as simple in style as the Virelais, it is hardly surprising to find a complete absence of compositions in $\frac{9}{8}$ time. As in the Ballades and Rondeaux, triple prolation gives way to duple in the later works, $\frac{2}{4}$ and $\frac{3}{4}$ predominating. Another late feature is the use of musical rhyme in both Refrain and Stollen in the Virelai *Moult sui de bonne heure née* (31). As in the Rondeaux, this trait is no doubt a borrowing from the Ballade. Melodic repetitions occur in other places, for instance in the three-part Virelai *Tres bonne et belle* (23), where a three-bar Cantus phrase is repeated a fifth higher almost 20 bars later. *En mon cuer* and *Se je souspir* (30) are interesting for their openings, in which the accompanying Tenors not only begin above the Cantus parts, but also start before or after them. This marks a break from the old rules of note-against-note counterpoint, in which the part above the Tenor was always at the fifth or octave above the Tenor and began simultaneously with it. Moreover, both Virelais are forerunners of the Passacaglia form, for their Tenors are based on constantly varied melodic formulas. *Se je souspir* has the very popular motif of a descending octave, while the Tenor of *En mon cuer* resembles a palindrome with its descent and ascent of a hexachord (Ex. 15).

Ex. 15

Tenor

In addition, motivic interest is as important in the Virelais as in the more complex Ballades and Rondeaux.[7] An obvious case is the two-part Virelai *Dame, mon cuer emportés* (29), whose Cantus is made up of four or five motifs. Rhythmically, the main ones are ♩ ♩ , ♫ ♩ ♩ , ♪♩ ♪♩ . ♩ ♪♩ ; but the melody of one may stray to the other, as with the popular auxiliary-note motif ♫ ♩ ♩ . ♪♩ ♪♩ . The Tenor is remarkable for its stress of the tonic and dominant, confirming an assessment of the mode as Hypodorian. The seven-syllable text lines are matched by neat four-bar phrases, sometimes extended by the two-bar phrases of the four-syllable lines. The rule that one line of text should normally be followed by a rest in the music is fairly strictly followed in this piece, though, as we have seen, the Virelais are more continuous in texture than the Lays.

Two of the monophonic Virelais (13 and 14) fall into a hybrid category in between the Virelai and the Ballade. Musically they are just like the other Virelais, but textually they consist of three four- or six-line stanzas with a two- or three-line Refrain. The characteristic ABA structure of the Virelai is missing, as is the Abgesang text usually sung to the music of the Refrain.

The most modern of the Virelais are the two last ones, with their more expansive phrases and rhythmically more flexible Tenors. The trend to have either one note per measure, or simply to borrow an occasional motif from the upper part, is replaced by a new method of composing longer Tenor phrases with varied rhythms and some use of syncopation. *Moult sui de bonne heure née* (31) has some quite lengthy melismas on the penultimate syllables of its Cantus phrases. *De tout sui si confortée* (32) has only one short melisma, but its tonal system is very clearly Hypodorian and its phrase structure is well organized. In fact the six-line Refrain is really divided into

[7] See *Acta Musicologica* xxvii, p. 53.

two very similar sections of three lines each. The very minor differences between them are mainly the first three or four notes of each section and the additional musical phrase which ends the second section. Essentially this is no more than a *clos* to the preceding *ouvert* phrase, which precedes it directly (Ex. 16).

Ex. 16

lie et jo - li - e pen-sé –   –   –   –   e,   tant com je   vi – vray.

IV

THE BALLADES AND RONDEAUX

The forty-two Ballades and twenty-one Rondeaux are doubtless the most distinctive and advanced contribution made by
Machaut to the art of composition. The standard poetic forms
outlined in Chapter 1 can, of course, be varied in a number of
ways, though the Ballade and Rondeau remain the classic
fixed forms of the fourteenth century. Occasionally Machaut's
Ballade stanzas have more than eight lines of text,[1] for instance *Doulz amis, oy mon compleint* (6) with fourteen lines,
though this can be considered as ten lines with internal
rhyme. The extension may be partly accounted for by the
musical form, which has both the second half as well as the
first half of the composition repeated with first and second
time bars. A similar case is *Amours me fait desirer* (19), which
has twelve-line stanzas, like the so-called Baladelle from the
Remède de Fortune. One of the most mature Ballades, which
also has this AABB musical form, departs entirely from the
Ballade stanza and adopts what Machaut elsewhere calls a
complainte form. This is the Ballade *Ma chiere dame* (40) with
sixteen lines in each stanza, consisting of four groups of four
lines, all decasyllables except the fourth line in each case, which
is a short line of four syllables. The rhyme scheme is aaab
up to the middle of the stanza and bbba from there to the end.
Unlike the other Ballades, the work has no poetic refrain either.
The economy measure of making the same music available
for at least two sections of text is of course paralleled in the
Lay and the Virelai.

[1] See *Musica Disciplina* xiii, p. 33.

Repetition of musical phrases is a natural means of formal unity in musical compositions, and the Ballade as cultivated by Machaut increasingly employs the technique known as musical rhyme, in which the end of the first half and the end of the second half of the work are musically identical. In the earlier works the identity may only extend to a few notes in each part, as in *Je ne cuit pas* (14), and is often not present at all. Later, however, it becomes a regular feature, and may comprise six or more bars. A good example is the melisma already quoted in Ex. 4, though the musical rhyme also applies to the other three parts as well.

If the composition of the Lays and Virelais is to some extent conditioned by the text, due to the predominantly syllabic nature of the settings, this is less true of the Ballades and Rondeaux, since relatively short texts are often spread over a great many notes. Melismas are likely to occur particularly at the beginning and end of principal sections in the Ballade, while in between we may find relatively syllabic writing, or more likely a half-and-half style in which there is usually more than one note per syllable. It is here that the ornamental motives come into play. Of course the Ballade stanzas are longer than the Rondeau refrains, which have an equivalent amount of music, and therefore an initial melisma is much more common in the Rondeaux.

A typical example of Machaut's earlier Ballades is *Pour ce que tous mes chans fais* (12), a two-part work in the Hypolydian mode of F. There is a suggestion of a modulation to B flat at the opening of the second half of the composition, but this may be caused by the leap from F in the Tenor down to B, which necessitates a flat to avoid the diminished fifth. The following E flats in Cantus and Tenor are then necessitated by the B flat of the Tenor.

The rhythm of the piece is $\frac{6}{8}$, using the major prolation typical of the early Ars Nova. It also tends to move in perfect or triple mode (*modus*). The Tenor in fact almost never moves in the short values of *prolatio*. An interesting feature which tends to confirm the presence of *modus* in this Ballade is the refrain *Se je chant mains que ne suel*, which is a borrowed one obviously in *modus perfectus*.[2] It was also used in the fourteenth century as the opening phrase of the *chace* with the same title, a remarkably mature three-part canon at the unison.[3] The presence of a borrowed refrain partly accounts for the lack of musical rhyme in this piece, but also, as we have seen, musical rhyme was less common in earlier works. The ornamental motifs are those we can find in many of the motets (Ex. 17).

Ex. 17

Harmonically the work is fairly simple, and, as in many parts of Machaut's Mass, it is easy to see the basic intervals beneath the ornamentation. Ex. 18 shows the opening of the second

Ex. 18

half of the Ballade, first with the Cantus as it is written, and second reduced to its basic note-against-note framework. No wonder theorists did not bother to give details of florid writing! The important thing was the underlying harmony, and it was left to the composer and practical performer to deal

---

[2] A thirteenth-century Virelai without music begins with this refrain (Oxford, Bodleian Libr., Douce ms 308, f. 225). The poem has been published in Gennrich's *Rondeaux, Virelais und Balladen* I, no. 171.

[3] This may well be Machaut's source. Up to now it has only been published as a two-part canon by H. Besseler, 'Studien zur Musik des Mittelalters I', *Archiv für Musikwissenschaft* VII (1925), p. 251.

with additional ornamental motifs. This was no doubt why Machaut in the *Voir Dit* told his beloved Péronne to sing his Ballade *Nès que on porroit* (33) without adding or taking away.[4]

Plourés, dames, the preceding Ballade in the complete works and also written for the *Voir Dit,* has much in common with *Nès que on porroit.* Although *Nès que on porroit* begins and ends in C, while *Plourés, dames* begins in C and ends in D Dorian, the thematic material and the $\frac{9}{8}$ time are common to both pieces. They even both have a one-bar solo interlude between phrases in the Tenor. Furthermore, they make frequent use of a particularly ornate form of the motif of a descending fourth or fifth in the Cantus (*a*), and introduce a syncopated motif (*b*) in the Tenor and Contratenor (Ex. 19).

Ex. 19

Both of these motifs fall into the category of integrative devices, but although they cannot easily be mistaken they are nearly always melodically differentiated. In the sequential passage quoted in Ex. 20 for instance, the general contour of formula 19a is repeated three times, but each time it is melodically varied. The repetition of the same motif, whether

Ex. 20

purely rhythmic or partly in melodic sequence, produces the most definite effect, as at the beginning of the Contratenor of *Plourés, dames,* where Ex. 19b occurs three times in succession. An almost isorhythmic effect is produced by the appearance of a single short motif (Ex. 21) in 15 out of 29 bars in the Ballade

[4] Ludwig II, p. 55 (*Voir Dit*, letter 10, p. 69).

Gais et jolis (35), but true isorhythm appears only in the first

of Machaut's Ballades: *S'Amours ne fait*. The imperfect *modus* and perfect prolation of this two-part work are an indication of its early date, and the isorhythm was no doubt an experiment inspired by Machaut's work in the motet field. Both Cantus and Tenor are isorhythmic, but there is a change of rhythm after the first and second time bars in the middle of the composition. Machaut has followed the verse scheme in arranging his *taleae*, two in the first half and three in the second half, corresponding to the two statements of two lines in the Stollen and three lines in the Abgesang of the seven-line Ballade. If rhythmic intricacies are the order of the day in Machaut's melismatic songs, genuine melodic sequences are almost non-existent, though there is a beautiful one in the early Ballade *Biauté qui toutes autres pere* (4) (Ex. 22).

Ex. 22

The Ballades in duple prolation employ similar motifs to those in triple, for instance ornamented forms of the descending fourth and fifth. They seem to make rather more use, however, of escape notes. The first half of the Cantus part of the four-part Ballade *Il m'est avis* (22) is almost a study on this motif. The more typical use of the motif appears in bar 20, but the opening of the piece is particularly interesting because it stresses the figure by augmentation. (Exx. 23a and b). Needless to say, the use of the motif does not necessarily involve the typical escape-note dissonance off the beat, for instance if the interval of a sixth follows that of a fifth between two parts. Also the figure typically represented by quavers, as in Ex. 23b, may resolve in the same direction as the movement of the

figure. It therefore becomes very much the same thing as passing notes.

The combination of duple time and duple prolation ($\frac{2}{4}$ or $\frac{4}{4}$) made syncopation a simple matter, and probably led to the complexities of late fourteenth-century syncopation in triple prolation, which is hardly ever anticipated in Machaut. The simplest syncopation in duple prolation is ♪ ♩ ♪, usually found in descending form, replacing ♩ ♩ harmonically. It can easily be extended over more notes, e.g. ♪♩ ♩ ♩ ♪; and also, because of the text it may be replaced by a repeated note, as in Ex. 24, where the second bar and the succeeding bar exemplify

Ex. 24

another substitution involving the ubiquitous auxiliary note ornament. Many variants of this technique are to be found, such as the replacement of the first note of a rhythmic syncopation by a rest, or its incorporation in the preceding dotted note. Elsewhere I have called these rhythmic shifts displacement technique, because it is evident that the composer began harmonically with the note-against-note harmonies and then shifted the material in one voice, usually the top one, a little to

the right or left. Ex. 25 is a good example from the Ballade
Tres douce dame que j'aour (24). The first version is the pre-
sumed note-against-note original, the second the syncopated
version. Syncopation appears to be the predominant factor in
the Ballade *Gais et jolis* (35). We have already noticed the

Ex. 25
(a)

(b)

tempus syncopation in the Tenor, but the most varied permuta-
tions of *prolatio* syncopation appear in the Cantus as well. The
Contratenor too makes full use of *prolatio* syncopation, though
mainly in the form of the basic figure ♪ ♩ ♪ , while the Cantus
involves full ⁴ measures in syncopation, usually with the falling
fifth interval divided by step.

It is hardly surprising to find great use of *prolatio* syncopation in the bitextual four-part Ballade *Quant Theseus—Ne quier
veoir* (34), which immediately precedes *Gais et jolis* in most of
the complete manuscripts. The Tenor is more animated in
Quant Theseus, but still has some bars of *tempus* syncopation.
In spite of their rhythmic independence, the Tenor and Contratenor together form a firm harmonic basis for the entire
composition, stressing the tonic and dominant of the mode, the
Ionian on C, in the process (Ex. 26). According to Machaut's
own account in the *Voir Dit*, the second poem *Ne quier veoir*
was composed by him as a counterpart to *Quant Theseus*,

which was the work of Thomas Paien. Froissart in his turn borrowed Machaut's poem when writing a work of his own which is very closely modelled on *Ne quier veoir*.[5]

Of the less usual Ballades, the tritextual *Sanz cuer m'en vois—Amis, dolens—Dame, par vous*[6] is a three-part canon at the unison. Here again there is much use of *prolatio* syncopation, though the measure is $\frac{3}{4}$. The modality of the piece is stressed by the emphasis on G and D, suggesting a transposed Dorian, judging by the frequent B flats. The other Ballade with three texts *De triste cuer—Certes, je di—Quant vrais amans* (29) is not canonic, though the thematic material has something in common with that of the preceding work. In addition, the escape note figure ♩ ♪♫ is frequently used, rather strikingly in the opening sequential phrase (Ex. 27). The four-part Ballade *En amer a douce vie* (41) from the *Remède de Fortune*, which has a rare example of syncopation in triple prolation in bar 4, also has a curious tonal scheme. The Cantus alone has a flat in the signature in the first half of the piece, while in the second the Cantus has two flats, the Tenors and Contratenor one, and the Triplum none. It would appear

---

[5] J. Froissart, *Poésies*, ed. A. Scheler (Brussels, 1871), II, p. 369; also Wilkins, *One Hundred Ballades, Rondeaux and Virelais*, p. 50.

[6] A correct transcription appears in *Acta Musicologica* xxvii (1955), p. 57.

that the first half of the piece is in the major mode of C; then, proceeding to the minor mode with a transition to B flat major, the piece ends in C minor (or Dorian twice transposed).

The modernity of the Rondeaux is indicated by the absence of triple prolation. Only 5 out of 22 compositions have it. Another early trait is the motet-like use of a Triplum rather than a Contratenor in the Rondeau from the *Remède* and in *Doulz viaire gracieus*, the first of the main Rondeau collection. There are no Rondeaux with more than one text, but three pieces are four-part works. Of these, both *Tant doucement* (9) and *Rose, liz* (10) are very mature compositions displaying not only excellent part-writing but very harmonious textures. Earlier works like the Ballade *En amer a douce vie* from the *Remède* often had dissonant clashes between the Cantus and the Triplum, but these are smoothed out in the two Rondeaux. Both of them also hover at times between two different types of measure, *Tant doucement* between $\frac{2}{4}$ and $\frac{3}{4}$, and *Rose, liz* between $\frac{3}{4}$ and $\frac{6}{8}$.[7] Ex. 28 is a good example of this fluidity in the latter work. Both *Rose, liz* and the final Rondeau of the collection, the three-part *Quant je ne voy ma dame* (21) have a very modern feature for a Rondeau, namely musical rhyme. Since the first half of the Rondeau must end on an inconclusive cadence and the second half on a conclusive one, the

<hr />

[7] See Günther, *Archiv für Musikwissenschaft* xix–xx, p. 18; Hoppin, *Musica Disciplina* xiv, p. 20.

musical rhyme cannot be complete, but it is extremely near it in *Quant je ne voy*, for it extends over fifteen measures of $\frac{2}{4}$ time. Another feature of these late works is more extended syncopation. Ex. 29 is an example from the Cantus part of

Ex. 29

Quant je ne voy which involves both *tempus* and *prolatio*.

The Rondeau *Ma fin est mon commencement* (14) is an unusual work. Both written parts are employed in 'retrograde' motion (perhaps this was the first time the term was used in the history of music). The upper part, however, is performed in its entirety in reverse with itself, making excellent two-part counterpoint. The Contratenor, on the other hand, is only half as long as the other part, and therefore it is performed in reverse from the middle of the composition, making not only a third part to the other two but an excellent bass line, with much stress on the tonic and dominant of C. Ex. 30 gives the ending of the piece.

The rhythmic complexities of this highly melismatic style suggest that such compositions like the motet, were intended

Ex. 30

primarily for audiences of intellectuals and the elite of the various princely courts. And if such subtleties sometimes appear a little 'precious' in the second half of the twentieth century, they also represent a tremendous advance on the inevitable triple time of the thirteenth century.

V

THE MOTETS

Owing to the relative complexity of the technique, it was necessary to give a fairly detailed account of the structure of the fourteenth-century motet in the chapter on Machaut's musical style. But the strangeness of this medieval form should not blind us to familiar features, as can easily happen when we see the almost mathematically precise arrangement of these pieces in a modern transcription. The lower parts look excessively long, and the upper ones seem to have little musical shape. Study of individual parts, however, often shows that the text determines the musical phrase almost as precisely in some Tripla and Moteti as in the Lays and Virelais.[1] Long notes and rests mark off the ends of lines of text just as they do in the more specifically secular forms, though the overlapping of the other parts may disguise this break. Two or more text lines are often joined without a break in the Tripla of such a continuously moving texture as that of the isorhythmic motet, but this does not invalidate the preceding statement. Ex. 31 is a phrase from the Triplum of the motet *De Bon Espoir—Puis que la douce—Speravi* (4), which consists of one decasyllabic line of text bounded at each end by one bar's rest. The statements of medieval writers like Aegidius de Murino have

Ex. 31

m'a · bonne A - mour · mein - tes · fois · se - cou - ru

[1] See Reichert.

tended to obscure this relation of text to music, for he seems to suggest that one should write the music first and then adapt the words to it as best one may.[2] Clearly, however, a poet as well-known as Machaut would not neglect the verse of his motets, and indeed this is fitted to the music very carefully, if often syllabically in the Triplum parts.

In the motet in question the Triplum proceeds in rhymed decasyllabic couplets throughout, in the pattern aabbccdd . . ., while the Motetus has a slightly more complex arrangement: seven-syllable lines with the pattern ababa ababa ababb. The Tenor of this three-part work has the melisma 'Speravi' from the Introit *Domine, in tua misericordia* for the first Sunday after Pentecost, which fits very well with the idea of the lover's hope in the French texts of the upper parts. The Tenor melody is stated twice, the second time in values diminished by a half, while each *color* is divided into three *taleae* each measuring 17 bars in length (i.e. 34 *tempus* bars in $\frac{6}{8}$). *Modus* and *tempus* are imperfect, prolation perfect, as so often in the motet.

Each *talea* of the Motetus comprises three lines of text, while the Triplum has twice as many lines with an overlap of one word from the succeeding section. The same procedure is followed in the second, diminished statement of the Tenor *color*, though naturally, with only half the number of measures, the Motetus *talea* has only two lines of text and the Triplum three. In other words, the organization of text and music could hardly be more perfectly related. Bridging the gap which would result between *taleae* if the textual and musical overlap were not considered, is a constant preoccupation of Machaut in the motets. In consequence, the opening of the piece often differs rhythmically and melodically from the succeeding sections, because its text begins 'at the beginning', while that of the following *talea* will probably begin earlier or later in at least one voice. A case which seems to contradict this statement

[2] Coussemaker, *Scriptorum* . . . III, p. 125.

is the motet *J'ay tant mon cuer—Lasse! je sui en aventure—Ego moriar pro te* (7), in which at least the three undiminished *taleae* have Triplum and Motetus texts which end together on the last bar. However, the rest at the beginning of the second and third *talea* in the Triplum delays the entry of the next line of text by one bar, and the length of the last note of the first *talea* in the Motetus makes it last into the first bar of the second *talea*. Even then, the next line of text in the Motetus has to wait a further full bar's rest to begin. On top of all this, there is a further irregularity in that the last two bars of each *talea* form only one third of the perfect *maximodus* measure implied by the Tenor (Ex. 32). The usual overlap occurs in

Ex. 32

II

any case in the Motetus in the diminished *taleae* which end the piece. Each *talea* contains two lines of text, but two syllables from the following line are sung before the beginning of the next *talea*. This ingenious technique, which applies to both French and Latin motets, is of course a development of the

Ars Antiqua method, whereby cadences are bridged by at least one voice, or the regularity of phrasing in one voice varied by a different phrasing in another (Ex. 33). Melodic

Ex. 33

repetition is not a common factor in Machaut's work, but it does occur in some motets, especially in the form of a refrain ending each *talea* of Motetus or Triplum. A particularly clear case occurs in the Triplum of *Quant vraie amour—O series summe rata—Super omnes speciosa* (17), in which the last line of each *talea* appears with the identical melodic phrase throughout, set off by rests preceding and following it. It is missing only in the final *talea*, which is shortened by five measures in order to avoid this phrase and make a more definite conclusion. This work is an example of the bilingual motet common in the thirteenth century but rare in the fourteenth. The Triplum text is French and that of the Motetus Latin, like the Tenor, a phrase from the Marian Antiphon *Ave, regina caelorum, ave, domina*. Once again the Tenor incipit *Super omnes speciosa* gives the key to the whole motet. The lady who is most beautiful of all is of course the Virgin Mary. Both Latin and French texts are couched in amorous language, but it is clear that the poet's love is a spiritual one.

Complete isorhythm occurs in only two of Machaut's motets (13, 15). In these the upper parts as well as the lower ones, i.e. Tenor and Contratenor, follow a scheme of identical rhythmic repetitions. Many of the other works, however, are

53

almost as restrictive, so that lengthy phrases in several succeeding *taleae* may be rhythmically identical. This is particularly true where hocketing or rests occur. Ex. 34 is a particularly

Ex. 34

interesting example of this technique, for the phrase is also
repeated within the *talea* as well as in each of the four *taleae*
proper. Interestingly enough, the reduction of the final *talea*
to eight *modus* measures instead of twelve eliminates this
repetition. This motet, *Tu qui gregem—Plange, regni—
Apprehende arma et scutum et exurge* (22) is one of the three
final Latin motets by Machaut which are in effect prayers for
peace at the time of the Hundred Years War, presumably
some time after 1356.

Many other technical procedures are used by Machaut in his
motets. Three of them follow thirteenth-century methods in
having a secular song as the Tenor, in one case a Rondeau and
in the others a Virelai. The folk-like nature of the Virelai made
it a natural choice as a basis for polyphonic compositions with
multiple texts through the fourteenth and fifteenth centuries.[3]
In the two motets whose Tenor texts have been preserved,
the three voices blend much better than in the isorhythmic
works. The huge length of the notes in the lower parts is less
apparent. The secular element comes through in *Trop plus est*

[3] See Reaney, 'Virelai B', *MGG* xiv, col. 1807.

bele—Biauté parée—Je ne sui mie (20) by the use of iambic as well as trochaic rhythms. In the two motets based on Virelais, it is the duple prolation which suggests the folk element. A striking feature of the former work is the way the middle part, the Motetus, suddenly moves into a higher range at bar 27, and continues above the Triplum till bar 37. One of the unifying features is a three-bar hocketing passage between Triplum and Motetus. This occurs three times in all, each time over a different segment of the frequently repeated Tenor. *Lasse! comment oublierary—Se j'aim—Pour quoy me bat mes maris?* (16) is noteworthy for the leaps in the Motetus. Even though leaps of a sixth and seventh occur between lines of the text, there is no break in the music at these points. Leaps of an octave occur too, both ascending and descending. In fact, the impression is that the Triplum was composed to the Tenor before the Motetus, though usually the reverse is the case. *Dame, je sui cilz—Fins cuers doulz* (11) is unusual in its use of triple time and duple prolation, though this combination occurs once more in Machaut's motets in the work for St. Quentin (19). The present piece, however, is also exceptional in its use of a quasi-imitative technique between Triplum and Motetus, often involving the use of a motif outlining the descending or ascending tetrachord. The method is undoubtedly related to that overlapping to be found at the beginning of *taleae* in the isorhythmic motets, since the imitation occurs at the start of a new phrase of the Virelai in the Tenor (Ex. 35).

As in the isorhythmic motets, so in those based on secular

Ex. 35

Tenors the concept of *modus* still holds sway, except in motet 20. It is this feature, no doubt, which in the isorhythmic motets leads to the use of another rhythmic element, diminution. Even in the Notre Dame organa of the late twelfth and early thirteenth centuries there had been a tendency to begin with a long-held Tenor and end with relatively short notes. In the fourteenth-century motet, the counterpart to this heightening of tension was the use of Tenor notes diminished by a half or a third in value, often combined with hocket in the upper parts. Thus, the second half of the piece positively skipped along to its conclusion. In keeping with Machaut's striving for variety in the motet, only ten compositions employ diminution, including both early and late works, which are however differentiated by shorter or longer *taleae* respectively. The organization of *De Bon Espoir—Puis que la douce—Speravi* has already been discussed, but a particularly interesting case is the four-part motet *Aucune gent—Qui plus aimme—Fiat voluntas tua* (5), whose Contratenor is the retrograde version of the Tenor, rather like the Cantus and Tenor of the Rondeau *Ma fin est mon commencement* (14). In addition, the Tenor is in imperfect *maximodus* against the Contratenor's perfect mensuration. The result is three notes in the Contratenor against two in the Tenor, each Tenor note equalling two measures of $\frac{9}{8}$ in the upper parts. Thus Machaut has effectively set two Tenor notes against three Contratenor notes against four measures of the upper parts. To add to the complexity, the roles of Contratenor and Tenor are reversed after every eight measures of the Triplum and Motetus. After four Tenor *taleae*, there are four *taleae* diminished by a half in the two lower parts. This means that two Tenor notes now correspond to two upper voice measures, so that the three Contratenor measures are still set against two notes of the Tenor, but against only two measures of the upper parts, instead of four. Ex. 36 shows the opening of the two halves of the composition.

Ex. 36

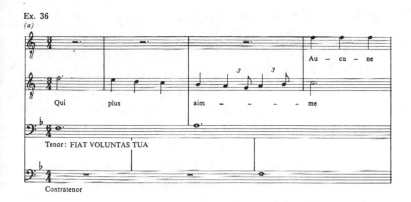

Among the unusual features of Machaut's motets are the so-called Introitus, i.e. preludes, which, in spite of their rhythm, fall outside the isorhythmic scheme of the rest of their respective pieces. Philippe de Vitry had no doubt introduced this practice, for it appears in no less than four motets attributed to him. As with Vitry, however, this usage is exceptional, though it appears in all five of the last motets by Machaut, apart from the Rondeau motet no. 20. The only other motet by Machaut with an Introitus is no. 9. The big difference between nos. 9 and 19 on the one hand and the last three motets on the other is that the presumably earlier pair involve only the Triplum as a solo, while the other works, though they tend to start as solos, gradually involve the Motetus and, in nos. 21 and 23, the Tenor and Contratenor as well. Actually, no. 22 is unusual in that the first voice to enter is the Motetus, while the Triplum just completes the Introitus cadence in a relatively short prelude. The really magnificent Introitus are those in nos. 21 and 23, which cover over 40 bars in $\frac{6}{8}$ time. As usual, Machaut is complete master of the rhythmic situation, and produces an aurally interesting clash between the imperfect *modus* of the upper parts, and the perfect *modus* with imperfect *maximodus* of the lower ones when they enter after 24 bars of motet 23.[4] (Ex. 37).

Ex. 37

[4] A further motet *Li enseignement de Chaton—De touz les biens—Ecce tu pulchra* is attributed to Machaut in the Fribourg fragment, Bibl. Cantonale et universitaire, Z 260, f. 86. It is published in Schrade I, p. 106 and by G. Zwick, p. 53. Its authenticity is doubted both by H. Besseler in Ludwig IV, p. 82 and Günther, *Musica Disciplina* xii, p. 32, note 23.

As with other types of composition, the mystery of how and when the motets were performed remains. Johannes de Grocheo said they were for the entertainment of the elite,[5] though he was writing slightly before the era of the Ars Nova. This may well be true of many of the French motets, but the Latin ones could have been substituted for or supplemented the concluding pieces of plainsong offices. A good example is Machaut's *Felix virgo—Inviolata* (23), based on the words of the Marian Antiphon *Salve regina* in the Tenor and clearly addressed to the Virgin Mary in the upper parts. It is easy to imagine the upper parts being performed by trained boy choristers, but the lower parts with their long notes would come off better on instruments. The organ was the principal instrument used in church in the Middle Ages, and might well have performed Tenor parts. A second organ could have been used for the Contratenor. In any case, whether voices or instruments were used for the Tenors and Contratenors, which were generally textless apart from the plainsong incipit in the Tenor, there was often a shortage of Contratenors, since quite a number of fourteenth-century motets have so-called Solus Tenor parts, which combine the Tenor and Contratenor into a single line.[6] Other instruments which could have been used in the lower parts are sackbuts, viols and probably shawms or rebecs.

[5] See E. Rohloff, *Der Musiktraktat des Johannes de Grocheo*, Leipzig, 1943, p. 56.

[6] See S. Davis, 'The Solus Tenor in the 14th and 15th Centuries', *Acta Musicologica* xxxix (1967), p. 44.

VI

THE MASS AND HOQUETUS

Machaut's Mass is his best-known composition today, not
without justification, for the work combines the best features of
his various styles. To compare it with other fourteenth-century
polyphonic Mass settings[1] is to realize how much better
Machaut's complete Ordinary is than other settings, usually of
isolated movements. He accepts the challenge of a complete
Mass in four-part harmony, whereas the other three complete
fourteenth-century Ordinaries[2] are in three parts throughout,
except for the Agnus of the Barcelona Mass.[3] Moreover, these
Masses do not give the impression of being created as a unit,
and certainly the Barcelona and Toulouse Masses contain
movements known elsewhere in isolation. Indeed, they have
one movement in common, the popular Credo *de rege* by the
composer Sortis.[4] The Tournai Mass is more unified, and has
some resemblance to the Machaut work in the Gloria and
Credo, though more in the latter than in the former movement.
The pervading triple prolation of the Tournai Gloria is familiar
from Machaut's motets but appears nowhere in his Mass.
Even so, Machaut's Gloria has a similarity to the Tournai

[1] See H. Stäblein-Harder, *Fourteenth-Century Mass Music in France* (Tübingen, 1962).

[2] The Barcelona, Toulouse and Tournai Masses are all published in Schrade I,
p. 139, 132 and 110; the first two Masses also by Stäblein-Harder, nos. 19, 25, 47, 56, 72
and in *Musica Disciplina* vii (1953), p. 119; the Tournai Mass also by Ch. van den Borren
Missa Tornacensis (Haarlem, 1957).

[3] This is in four parts. The incomplete Sorbonne Mass now preserved at the Insti-
tut de Musicologie of the University of Paris has the Kyrie, Gloria and Sanctus in three
parts, and the Agnus and Benedicamus in only two (see J. Chailley, 'La Messe de Besan-
çon et un compositeur inconnu du XIVe siècle', *Annales Musicologiques* II (1954), p. 93).

[4] Schrade I, p. 150; Stäblein-Harder, no. 47.

Gloria in its use of a relatively note-against-note texture, and because of the method of progression: more or less ornamented chordal measures in crotchets, ending each time with a full-measure chord. After an important phrase ending, there may be a link passage in which one or more parts rest. Exx. 38a and b from the two Credos however, are much more revealing. Clearly Machaut or the Tournai composer knew the other man's work. Yet, while the Tournai composer continues the

Ex. 38
(a) (Machaut)

(b) (Tournai)

Amen in exactly the same style, Machaut writes an isorhythmic peroration which combines hocket with syncopation in a lively affirmation of faith. Both upper and lower pairs of voices engage in the trick of exchanging rhythms. If, therefore,

Machaut was obeying the Bull of Pope John XXII in setting his main text syllabically in all four parts,[5] he abandoned this principle with a vengeance when all he had to set was the one word Amen. Ex. 39 shows the ending of it. To be sure, there

Ex. 39

was some chordal ornamentation, and this resulted, at the words 'Et vitam venturi seculi' preceding the Amen, in a sublime series of dissonant harmonies, all created by the Contratenor (Ex. 40).

Ex. 40

Whatever other features affect the music, however, it is the text and its syllabic setting which give the Gloria and Credo their impetus. The use of duple *tempus* and *prolatio* gives a

[5] H. Harder, 'Johann XXII', *MGG* vii, col. 83.

fluidity which is not to be found in the Lays and Virelais. The basic $\frac{2}{4}$ can be combined into groups of $\frac{4}{4}$ and $\frac{3}{2}$ which themselves are grouped into larger sections suited to the text phrases. The opening and closing syllables of a phrase are usually set to long notes, and the intermediate syllables to shorter ones, as in Ex. 38. This verbal declamation is well balanced, and as so often in Machaut, there is frequently a relation of two bars of declamation (i.e. short notes) to one bar of rest, usually a single long note. Where one declamatory bar is followed by one bar of relaxation, there is often a further phrase of the same kind, as in Ex. 40. Very short notes, represented by quavers in the modern transcription, are rare but effective when they do occur, as at the words 'simul adoratur et conglorificatur'.

This 'simultaneous' style is not unknown in other four-teenth-century Mass settings, but Otto Gombosi was the first to penetrate the formal plan of Machaut's Gloria and Credo.[6] He calls it strophic. The Gloria is the simpler of the two movements, and begins with a five-bar chordal prelude to the words 'Et in terra pax'. The four stanzas ('hominibus . . . gloriam tuam,' 'Domine deus . . . filius patris', 'Qui tollis . . . miserere nobis', 'Quoniam tu solus sanctus . . . dei patris') are each divided into three subsections, ending respectively on a half-cadence, a full cadence and another full cadence. In each case the link passage for Tenor and Contratenor only follows the second subsection, so that the listener is made aware that, although he has heard a full close, he is not yet at the end of the stanza. Another refinement is to be found in stanza 3, where the two-part link occurs after the half-cadence, while, after the second subsection, the link is expanded to four voices and given the text 'Qui sedes'. The Amen of the Gloria is not isorhythmic, though there are many rhythmically identical phrases, usually in successive bars or

---

[6] *Musical Quarterly* xxxvi, p. 209.

pairs of bars. An example of this technique, which involves both hocket and syncopation, is given in Ex. 41.

Ex. 41

The Credo is even more complex in strophic structure. It consists essentially of three large sections, which are divided into three smaller ones, each of these again comprising either four or five short phrases. The two-part link passages usually appear at the end of the smaller sections, e.g. 1, 2, 4, 7, 8. The omission at section 5 is repaired by the appearance of the link after the second phrase of section 6. Such are the subtleties of construction to be found in this work. The Amen of the Credo is isorhythmic and textless, but it nevertheless continues the ratio of one bar of relaxation to one of activity which we found in the syllabic sections (cf. Ex. 39).

The fully isorhythmic movements of the Mass are those with relatively short texts (Kyrie, Sanctus, Agnus, and Ite). As in some of the latest motets, the Sanctus and Agnus have a prelude outside the isorhythmic scheme. The three initial invocations of the Sanctus are each five bars in length and the third is identical with the first. The intention is no doubt to emphasize the change of tonality from the Dorian mode of the first three movements to the Lydian of the last three. There is a further point of formal interest in the fact that the first bar of the succeeding phrase 'dominus deus Sabaoth' precedes the first bar of the isorhythmic *talea*. In a similar asymmetric fashion, the initial syllable of the Benedictus is set to the last bar of a *talea*. The Agnus, instead of having a prelude consisting of three phrases, has one six-bar phrase at the beginning of each of the three Agnus sections, each phrase preceding a two-*talea* isorhythmic section. It is noteworthy, too, that, as in the Sanctus, the first Agnus prelude is followed by a single bar of the succeeding text phrase preceding the isorhythmic scheme. The outer movements of the Mass, on the other hand, have no preludes.

The Kyrie, which borrows its Tenor from the Vatican Mass IV (*Cunctipotens*), gradually expands its *taleae* from four to fourteen measures of major *modus*. Each measure is represented in modern transcription by a dotted semibreve. The most noteworthy feature of all four sections of the complete movement is the retention of the rigid third rhythmic mode pattern of Kyrie I in the other *taleae*, though with modifications. In fact, Kyrie I can be considered as having two larger *taleae* of twelve measures plus a coda, since this *talea* fits the Contratenor and, more freely, the upper parts. Similarly, the final Kyrie can be thought of as having *taleae* of seven measures in multiples of two, though again the rhythm is less fixed than in the fourteen-measure groups. Ex. 42 shows a *talea* from each of the four sections of the movement. Apparently the number of statements of the text, and hence of the musical sections, is the same as in the plainsong Kyrie, namely three of Kyrie I, three of the Christe, two of Kyrie II, and one of Kyrie III.

The Tenor melodies of the Sanctus and Agnus are both taken from Vatican Mass XVII. The Sanctus has ten statements of a single eight-measure *talea*, which however is curtailed on the final statement to six measures. The interesting feature of the individual *taleae* is the clear division of the four-part setting into $2+1+2+1+2$ measures, in which the single bars are a chord of relaxation. Also the central two measures

Ex. 42

are some of the most active in the whole Mass in the upper parts. The Triplum hockets very quickly in a complementary rhythm to the Motetus, which employs both *tempus* and *prolatio* syncopation (Ex. 43). The Agnus has a more continuous

Ex. 43

texture in invocations I and III, which are musically identical, though there is again plenty of activity in the upper parts, with a good deal of triadic melodic movement in syncopated passages. Agnus II is particularly well organized, however, and is reminiscent of such motets as *Tu qui gregem—Plange, regni* (22) in that it divides the individual *talea* in all four parts into three isorhythmic sub-sections. The Ite, as might be expected, is a shorter movement based on two eight-measure *taleae* setting the melody of the Magnificat Antiphon *O quam suavis*, which is also used as the plainsong Sanctus of Vatican Mass VIII. The syncopation and hocket of the upper parts is reminiscent of the Agnus I.

The remaining isorhythmic work of Machaut is the isolated Hoquetus. Not only is it unique in Machaut's output, but no other example can be found in the whole of fourteenth-century music. It was really an offshoot of the thirteenth-century motet, and therefore tends to be based on a plainsong Tenor, in this case the melisma 'David' from the Alleluia verse *Nativitas gloriose virginis*.[7] If this is another text in honour of the Virgin Mary, like the Mass, we may doubt that it was used in church. More likely it falls once again into the category of entertainment for the intellectual community of the church or the nobility. There are two different methods of organizing the Tenor. The first is a series of eleven-bar *taleae* with even notes in the first four bars and some hocketing in the last six. The melody overlaps with this scheme, so that there are three *colores* to eight *taleae*. The latter part of the piece consists simply of what the fourteenth-century theorist Egidius de Murino called a *tenor ordinatus*,[8] namely a series of even notes followed by a rest. In this case there is only one statement of the melody and four nine-bar *taleae*, of which the last one lacks the final rest. In this part of the composition, therefore, the Tenor has just one note per measure. Harmonically the piece is quite remarkable because of the way the parts cross. The sudden appearance of a third in a perfect consonance such as the fifth gives a harmonic pungency quite as effective as a dissonance, but dissonances too are created in the same way, i.e. by the insertion of a note into a chord after a rest in that part, in other words by hocket. A particularly striking example occurs as a climax near the end, where the

---

[7] Now called *Solemnitas gloriose virginis*.
[8] Coussemaker, *Scriptorum* . . . III, p. 125.

final *talea* begins with a held third, and, after a crotchet rest, the middle part of the three enters with a seventh in a very exposed position. This resolves in the following bar to a fifth, after a rest in hocket fashion (incidentally creating a unison). Then, in the succeeding bar, the effect of another seventh is created by the sudden entry of the highest part with a low G. The actual chord is a triad, but since the middle part has only just moved from a stressed F sharp, the resulting effect is that of a major seventh. No doubt Machaut was really aiming at the effect of a resolution from F sharp to G., but the way he does it is somewhat unusual (Ex. 44).

Ex. 44

CONCLUSION

When we consider the various aspects of Machaut's output, the conviction grows that he is perhaps the earliest composer to emerge as an outstanding writer in the modern sense, in that he cultivated the leading forms of his own time. Before him, composers either wrote songs or church music. Machaut did both, though it could be said that he neglected the area of liturgical church music with the principal exception of the four-part Mass, and possibly a handful of Latin motets. The motet, however, though the foremost form of composition in the early fourteenth century, was often secular, even when written in Latin, and most of Machaut's motets have French texts.

Amongst Machaut's predecessors, Adam de la Hale seems to have been the only composer to have approached him in range, writing both polyphonic Rondeaux and motets, as well as an important body of monophonic song.[1] By comparison, however, Adam's motets are conservative works in the typical thirteenth-century $\frac{3}{4}$ rhythm, though the highest part of the three, in particular, often has triplet quavers which may be set to separate syllables of the text, as in *Adieu quemant—Aucun se sont loé*.[2] The 16 three-part Rondeaux are unique, but again not especially modern. All are in $\frac{3}{4}$ measure, and, though the crotchets are divided into triplet quavers, there is no attempt to set each group to more than one syllable of text. The rhythmic principle is also still that of the rhythmic modes,

---

[1] Cf. the complete edition of his lyric works by N. Wilkins (Tübingen, 1967).

[2] Y. Rokseth, *Les Polyphonies du XIIIe siècle* III (Paris, 1936), p. 103; also Wilkins, *Adam de la Hale, Lyric Works*, p. 60.

mainly the first and second (trochaic or iambic). The note-against-note harmony, however, has an English sound reminiscent of some fourteenth-century compositions in discant style. Adam's works, even so, belong clearly to the Ars Antiqua tradition, while the contemporaries Vitry and Machaut belong to a different era.

Philippe de Vitry's reputation as the flower of musicians of his time is hard to maintain or deny, in view of the few works which can be attributed to him—some 12 or 13 motets,[3] plus a motet text and an isolated Ballade text,[4] which at least proves that he did write some secular songs. Unlike Machaut, he wrote his motets mainly in Latin, and, apart from the work in praise of Pope Clement VI, the subject-matter is far from sacred. Indeed, Vitry seems to have specialized in texts attacking enemies of the church and state, like *Cum statua Hugo*.[5] With Machaut we have the evidence of his complete works that he was in the forefront of the development of polyphonic song. Nevertheless, Vitry's motets are all of real quality, and betray the firm hand of the leader who realized that he was indeed writing a 'new' type of music. The treatise *Ars nova*[6] is in fact concerned entirely with the writing of motets; one version is entitled *ars quaevis mensurandi motetos*, or 'the old and new arts of notating motets in mensural notation'. None of Vitry's motets are fully isorhythmic, but they are nevertheless just as up to date as Machaut's. The canonic opening, used by Dufay long after Vitry, is unknown to Machaut, though he uses canon at the unison in his Lays. Melodic sequence is much more common in Vitry: his motet *Petre Clemens—Lugentium*[7] has

[3] All published in Schrade I.
[4] Cf. E. Pognon, 'Ballades mythologiques', *Humanisme et Renaissance* V (1938), p. 409.
[5] Schrade I, 1954, p. 82.
[6] G. Reaney, A. Gilles and J. Maillard, 'The Ars Nova of Philippe de Vitry', *Musica Disciplina* X (1956), p. 13ff (also in book form as *Philippe de Vitry, Ars Nova*, Nijmegen 1964, p. 13ff).
[7] Schrade I, p. 97.

this as well as the canonical opening. Hocket too is more obvious and regular in Vitry than in Machaut, especially in the impressive 43-measure textless conclusion to the motet *Impudenter—Virtutibus*.[8] Moreover, Vitry stresses the major mode, Ionian or Lydian, in nearly all his motets. Both Machaut and Vitry are great craftsmen in their motets, but Machaut's is the more feminine art, for it is impossible to miss Vitry's strength and masculinity.

It is not easy to decide which are the most emotionally expressive works of Machaut. We have different criteria from the Middle Ages, even though Machaut is clearly a keen critic of his own work. When he says in the *Voir Dit* that some of his songs are sweet,[9] this may be a more astringent sweetness than we recognize, though the Ballades and Rondeaux of the *Voir Dit* may surely be counted among his best. Like anyone else, he matured as he continued to compose, and the last four motets, the polyphonic Lays, and such Rondeaux as *Tant doucement* (9) and *Rose, liz* (10) may be considered among his best works. Many of the Virelais are relatively early compositions, and no doubt appeal today because of their simplicity and more folklike sound, as compared with the melismatic, rhythmically complex phrases of the Ballades and Rondeaux. The Mass is a fine work, but its popularity today may be partly accounted for by its unusual harmonies. And yet it too shows masterly craftsmanship, both in its isorhythmic and its song-style movements, not to mention the tonal unity of three minor and three major movements. Perhaps this craftsmanship is what we come back to most of all, for it permeates all facets of Machaut's music: melody, rhythm, harmony, tonality, counterpoint, and thus continually suggests new points of interest.

Machaut is certainly a Janus-like figure, for his works point both backwards and forwards. The Lays were the swansongs

[8] ibid, p. 91.
[9] P. Paris, *Le Voir Dit*, pp. 69, 265.

of the genre, even though poets continued at least to recommend the verse-form in the fifteenth century.[10] And hockets, together with motets based on Tenors in Rondeau or Virelai form, belong to the thirteenth century. But the polyphonic Ballades and Rondeaux were known throughout Europe, and these had a tremendous influence on Machaut's immediate successors.[11] A composer like Landini was evidently moved to write many of his three-part Ballate after the manner of Machaut's polyphonic songs. *Donna'l tuo partimento*,[12] for instance, has many of Machaut's typical duple rhythm syncopations. In general, however, Landini's texture is smoother than Machaut's, in spite of his frequent use of the popular French $\frac{6}{8}$ rhythm, known in Italian as *senaria gallica*. Even in the gigantic Cyprus codex of the early fifteenth century, we can find Ballades like *Pymalion qui moult subtilz estoit*[13] which echo Machaut's style in both poetry and music. And Machaut's renown was stressed by Eustache Deschamps in his lament on the composer's death, set to music by F. Andrieu.[14] The impact of Machaut's work on the composers who immediately succeeded him is particularly clear in the polyphonic songs of Senleches, Solage, and others.[15] The rhythmic complexities and extensive syncopations of their works go back to Machaut's more modest practice. What he had done in duple rhythms, they carried forward in the more complicated triple rhythms of $\frac{6}{8}$ and $\frac{9}{8}$, particularly in the field of syncopation. Similarly, by developing the use of coloured notation and introducing various signs of measure and proportion, they made a very fluid, almost rubato melodic line possible, often using different

[10] E. Langlois, *Recueil d'Arts de Seconde Rhétorique* (Paris, 1903), pp. 17, 166.

[11] Cf. G. Reaney, 'Machaut's Influence on Late Medieval Music', *Monthly Musical Record* lxxxviii (1958), pp. 50ff, 96ff.

[12] Schrade IV, 1958, p. 106.

[13] R. H. Hoppin, *The Cypriot-French Repertory of the Manuscript Torino, Biblioteca Nazionale, J.II.9* III (Rome, 1963), p. 67.

[14] Modern edition by F. Ludwig, *Guill. de Machaut, Mus. Werke* I, p. 49.

[15] Cf. W. Apel, *French Secular Music of the Late Fourteenth Century* (Cambridge, Mass., 1950), nos. 34, 47–51, etc.

measures simultaneously in at least two voices.[16] Machaut had anticipated the latter technique in his motet *Felix virgo—Inviolata* (23), in which the Tenor has duple *modus* when the Contratenor has triple, and vice versa. The isorhythmic motet enjoyed a long life, for it only began to wane in popularity after the period of Dufay, who wrote one of his most famous motets *Nuper rosarum flores*[17] for the consecration of the cathedral in Florence in 1436. Vitry and Machaut established the form, which astounded their contemporaries by its rapidly moving upper parts, the hocket and scientifically established form. Few composers between Machaut and Dufay could neglect it, and even in Italy, where a freer motet was composed, men like Antonio de Civitate and Johannes Ciconia wrote isorhythmic motets.[18] The main change from the early to the later motet was the use of isorhythm in the upper as well as the lower parts. This too was anticipated by Machaut in two cases, as we have seen.

'I am but small of stature', said Machaut in his autobiographical poem *Le Voir Dit*.[19] At long last we are beginning to appreciate his emotional intensity as well as his craftsmanship, whether in the excitement of the motets or in the tenderness of Ballades like *Ma chiere dame*. Viewed from this distance we can only find his achievement, so far from small, uniquely impressive.

---

[16] ibid., no. 49.

[17] H. Besseler, *Guillelmi Dufay, Opera Omnia* I (Rome, 1966), p. 70.

[18] Ch. van den Borren, *Polyphonia Sacra* (Burnham, 1932), p. 188; S. Clercx, *Johannes Ciconia* II (Brussels, 1960), nos. 33, 39, 42.

[19] P. Paris, *Le Voir Dit*, p. 19.

CHRONOLOGICAL TABLE OF COMPOSITIONS
BY MACHAUT*

Compositions	Date
Motet 18	1324
Motet 19	1335
Lays 1–8	Before 1349
Ballades 1–16	Before 1349
Virelais 1–15, 17–21	Before 1349
7 compositions from the *Remède de Fortune*	Before 1349
Lay 16	1349
Lays 9–11, 13	1349–63
Motets 1–20	1349–63
Mass	1349–63
Hoquetus	1349–63
Ballades 17–31, 35	1349–63
Rondeaux 1–12, 14, 15	1349–63
Virelais 16, 22–30	1349–63
Lay 12	Before 1357
Motets 21–3	After 1356
Ballade 32	*c.* 1360–1
Rondeau 13 (Cantus)	After Christmas, 1361
Rondeau 13 (Tenor and Contratenor)	April 1363
Lay 13	End of June, 1363
Rondeau 16	October 27, 1363
Ballade 33	End of 1363
Ballade 34	November 3, 1363
Ballade 36	End of 1363
Lay 15	After 1363
Ballade 38	1363–71
Rondeaux 17–19	1363–71
Virelais 31–2	1363–71
Lays 17–18	*c.* 1367–77
Ballades 39–40	*c.* 1371–2
Rondeau 20	*c.* 1371–2

*Reproduced by kind permission of Dr. Armen Carapetyan

BIBLIOGRAPHY

Editions

Complete: F. Ludwig, *Guillaume de Machaut, Musikalische Werke*, 4 vols. (Leipzig and Wiesbaden, 1926–54).
L. Schrade, *Polyphonic Music of the Fourteenth Century*, vols. II–III (Monaco, 1956).
Separate pieces:
J. Chailley, *Guillaume de Machaut, Messe Notre-Dame* (Paris, 1948).
M. Hasselmann and T. Walker, 'More Hidden Polyphony in a Machaut Manuscript', *Musica Disciplina* xxiv (1970), p. 7.
R. H. Hoppin, 'An Unrecognized Polyphonic Lai of Machaut', *Musica Disciplina* xii (1958), p. 93.
A. Machabey, *La messe à quatre voix de Guillaume de Machaut* (Liège, 1948).
G. de Van, *Guillaume de Machaut, Double Hoquet* (Paris, 1938).
G. de Van, *Guglielmi De Mascandio Opera I: La Messe de Notre Dame* (Rome, 1949).
G. Zwick, 'Deux motets inédits de Philippe de Vitry et de Guillaume de Machaut', *Revue de Musicologie* xxx (1948), p. 28.

Books and Articles

Poetry:

V. Chichmaref, *Guillaume de Machaut, Oeuvres lyriques*, 2 vols. (Paris and St. Petersburg, 1909).
E. Hoepffner, *Oeuvres de Guillaume de Machaut*, 3 vols. (Paris, 1908–21).
P. Paris, *Le Voir Dit* (Paris, 1875).

Books and Articles

W. Dömling, *Die mehrstimmigen Balladen, Rondeaux und Virelais von Guillaume de Machaut* (Tutzing, 1970).
H. H. Eggebrecht, 'Machauts Motette Nr. 9', *Archiv für Musikwissenschaft* xix–xx (1962–63), p. 281; xxv (1968), p.173.
O. Gombosi, 'Machaut's Messe Notre-Dame', *Musical Quarterly* xxxvi (1950), p. 204.
U. Günther, 'Chronologie und Still der Kompositionen Guillaume de Machauts', *Acta Musicologica* xxxv (1963), 96 ff.

U. Günther, *Der musikalische Stilwandel der französischen Liedkunst in der zweiten Hälfte des 14. Jahrhunderts* (unpublished dissertation, Hamburg, 1957).

U. Günther, 'The 14th-Century Motet and its Development', *Musica Disciplina* xii (1958), p. 27.

U. Günther, 'Die Mensuralnotation der Ars nova in Theorie und Praxis', *Archiv für Musikwissenschaft* xix–xx (1962–3), p. 9.

R. H. Hoppin, 'Notational Licences of Guillaume de Machaut', *Musica Disciplina* xiv (1960), p. 13.

F. Blume, ed., *Die Musik in Geschichte und Gegenwart* (*MGG*), 14 vols. (Kassel and Basel, 1949–68).

A. Machabey, *Guillaume de Machault 130?–1377*, 2 vols. (Paris, 1955).

J. Maillard, *Evolution et Esthétique du Lai Lyrique* (Paris, 1963).

G. Reaney, 'A Chronology of the Ballades, Rondeaux and Virelais Set to Music by Guillaume de Machaut', *Musica Disciplina* VI (1952), p. 33.

G. Reaney, 'Ars Nova', *Pelican History of Music* I (1960), p. 261.

G. Reaney, 'Ars Nova in France', *New Oxford History of Music* III (1960), p. 1.

G. Reaney, 'Fourteenth Century Harmony and the Ballades, Rondeaux and Virelais of Guillaume de Machaut', *Musica Disciplina* VII (1953), p. 129.

G. Reaney, 'Guillaume de Machaut: Lyric Poet', *Music and Letters* xxxix (1958), p. 38.

G. Reaney, 'The Lais of Guillaume de Machaut and their *Background*', *Proceedings of the Royal Musical Association* lxxxii (1955), p. 15.

G. Reaney, 'The Ballades, Rondeaux and Virelais of Guillaume de Machaut: Melody, Rhythm and Form', *Acta Musicologica* xxvii (1955), p. 40.

G. Reaney, 'The Poetical Form of Machaut's Musical Works I', *Musica Disciplina* xiii (1959), p. 25.

G. Reaney, 'Towards a Chronology of Machaut's Musical Works', *Musica Disciplina* xxi (1967), p. 87.

G. Reaney, 'Voices and Instruments in the Music of Guillaume de Machaut', *Revue Belge de Musicologie* x (1956), p. 3 and 93.

G. Reichert, Das Verhältnis zwischen musikalischer und textlicher Struktur in den Motetten Machauts', *Archiv für Musikwissenschaft* xiii (1956), p. 197.

Connor could no longer see what was happening, but he heard a crunch of gears. When it came to piloting a boat, Ling was clearly more adept at speed than steering. The tender's engine roared, and the hull stopped within a fraction of Connor's head.

"Switch off the engine," shouted Brad, "before the propeller chops him into sushi."

He leaned over the bow rail and offered Connor a broad grin. "That was a close shave in more ways than one, wasn't it?"

By the time Ling appeared to help pull him aboard, the boat had drifted and Connor was once again beyond reach.

"You'll have to make another pass," said Brad.

Ling let out an exasperated sigh. She returned to the helm, started the engine and put it into reverse.

"No," said Brad. "If you go astern, you're in danger of butchering him."

"Why can't he just swim to us?" said Ling, her jaw set with frustration.

There was another crunch of gears. Brad raised his eyes to heaven, and Ling caught him in the act.

"Don't you dare say anything!" she muttered, hammering at the gears.

"Heaven forbid," replied Brad with his most guileless expression.

After three further attempts, Ling finally managed to

and the rushing thunder of water in his ears and eyes momentarily disoriented him. Brad had warned them both that any man-overboard situation was potentially fatal. Drowning, exposure, hypothermia and impact injury were all very real risks, especially if the person wasn't wearing a life jacket. Fortunately, Connor was, and he rapidly floated back to the surface. By the time his head cleared the water, Ling had cut back on the throttle and was starting to make a controlled turn toward him.

As the tender approached, Ling tried to keep a fix on his location. He'd already drifted farther out to sea with the current, and it would be easy to lose sight of a head bobbing in the water, even in a little swell.

"Slow down," Brad warned Ling. "You're approaching too fast."

Ling cut back on the throttle, but it was too little too late.

"Careful!" said Brad. "You're going to run over him."

Ling tried to correct the tender's direction, but without enough power, the rudder responded too slowly. The fiberglass hull cut through the water on a direct collision course with Connor's head.

"Go astern," Brad ordered as Connor, unable to dive because of the life jacket, held up his arms to shield himself.

"Astern? What's astern?" cried Ling, her voice rising in pitch as the tender plowed toward Connor.

"*Reverse!*"

pull alongside Connor and safely haul him aboard single-handedly.

"Well, we got there in the end," said Brad, patting a seething Ling on the shoulder. "But I think we need a bit more practice at the man-overboard drill, don't you?"

He raised an eyebrow at Connor, who stood dripping wet on the deck.

"Are you willing to throw yourself over for another drill?"

"Sure," said Connor. "But only if Ling promises not to try to run me over again."

Ling narrowed her eyes at him. "Well, hotshot, maybe next time I'll leave you to the sharks!"

28

"Pirates always hold the advantage," explained Brad, leaning forward and resting his elbows on the table in the sky lounge. "As the hunter, they choose the time and place. And, of course, they know that a yacht like this is virtually defenseless."

"But what about NATO's counterpiracy operation?" asked Connor.

"Yeah," said Ling, through a mouthful of tuna salad. "They've got warships that can protect us."

Brad laughed, a deep booming sound as loud as a foghorn. "That naval task force is pretty much useless! It's not their fault, mind you. With just one small fleet in an ocean this size, it's like a single police car trying to patrol the whole of France. An impossible task. Therefore, at sea we're on our own. And we must be prepared to defend ourselves."

The week of intensive MARSEC training had flown by. The two of them were now proficient in reading radar, interpreting